ACCLAIM FOR
SMART QUESTIONS TO ASK YOUR STOCKBROKER

"If you're looking for the inside story—as a first-time investor, occasional dabbler, or sophisticated financier—this is the one book you really need!"
> —Caroline Vanderlip, Senior Vice President, Affiliate Relations, CNBC

"An absolute 'must read' for everyone who wants to win in the world of investing."
> —Steve Crowley, TV money expert and author of *Money for Life*

"A practical, informative book for every investor. I wish I'd read it years ago."
> —Robert L. Shook, co-author, *The IBM Way* and *The Winner's Circle: How Ten Stockbrokers Became the Best in the Business*

D1531247

Other books in the *Smart Questions* series

Smart Questions to Ask Your Doctor
Smart Questions to Ask Your Lawyer
Smart Questions to Ask Your Insurance Agent

Published by
HarperPaperbacks

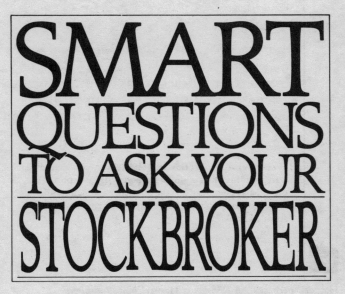

SMART QUESTIONS TO ASK YOUR STOCKBROKER

DOROTHY LEEDS
WITH JOAN ORAZIO AND
LAWRENCE B. GREENBAUM

HarperPaperbacks
A Division of HarperCollinsPublishers

aq5429

HarperPaperbacks   *A Division of* HarperCollins*Publishers*
10 East 53rd Street, New York, N.Y. 10022

Cover design by Richard Rossiter

First printing: April 1993

Printed in the United States of America

HarperPaperbacks and colophon are trademarks of HarperCollins*Publishers*

❖ 10 9 8 7 6 5 4 3 2 1

I dedicate this book to Gerry Miller, a wonderful friend, supporter, and expert in all aspects of finance and management.

ACKNOWLEDGMENTS

Special appreciation to:
My husband, Nonny Weinstock, who has so wisely invested for me, and in me, all these years.
Ron Greenbaum, a brilliant investor and inspiration.
Karen Solem, a great lady and a great editor.

Joan Orazio and I both want to express our appreciation for Sharyn Kolberg, whose expertise and excellent writing ability have added so much to this project.

Joan Orazio also says thank you to:
Lou Orazio, for his love and support through the years.
Paul V. Orazio, CFP, and Louise O. Mason, CFP, who lent their expertise to formulating clear, concise answers to some tough questions.
The staff of Orazio Financial Services, and especially Executive Assistant Dawn McKelvey for their patience and dedication to meeting deadlines.
All of my family and friends whose constant encouragement has helped me achieve my goals.

CONTENTS

INTRODUCTION

More than ever, investments are playing an important part in every family's financial future. In the past, you would work 25 or 30 years for one company, get a pension when you retired, add that to your Social Security and the money you'd been putting aside in your savings account every week, and live out your retirement years in comfort. Those times are gone forever.

Now, because of the complicated economic times in which we live, you must begin to prepare for your future earlier and earlier. A simple bank savings account won't suffice in these highly inflationary times. You know you must invest your money—but where, how, and with whom? How do you even know where to begin? A recent article in the the *New York Times* stated, "In an era of program trading, leveraged buyouts and trading volatility, novice . . . investors are at an extreme disadvantage." How do you take yourself out of the "novice investor" category? How do you know what kind of investments are best for you? You don't know . . . unless you ask questions!

Knowing the right questions can significantly reduce the risk a potential investor takes. We need accurate and up-to-date information that goes beyond the usual industry hype; only by asking careful questions can we begin to get the kind of information we need. However, because the financial services industry is growing so rapidly, it has become increasingly complicated and confusing. There are so many options from which to choose, it's hard to know which ones are right for you. You might feel pressured to make sound financial choices—not just for yourself, but for your family as well.When you're faced with these difficult choices and are feeling the pressure, you're likely to feel frightened as well; you don't ask as many questions as you should. Consequently, you don't get the information you need.

Yet this is just the time you need all the information you can get. You're probably being asked to make difficult decisions—decisions that may affect the rest of your life, and the lives of your family members as well.

Making investments used to mean a choice between investing in the stock market and buying real estate. Nowadays, however, there are literally hundreds of investment choices you can make to save for your kids' education, to add to your retirement fund, or to ensure the future of your business. When you are dealing with issues of this magnitude, it is your right, as well as your responsibility, to obtain the best possible information for your present and future well-being.

There's no need to let others have control over your financial affairs, to allow anyone else to make decisions for you, or to feel that you are a victim of coercion or circumstance. The purpose of this book is to provide you with the right questions to ask, and to increase your knowledge about the ingredients of a comfortable financial plan of investment. It is important to understand who you are as an investor and what kinds of risks you are willing—and able—to take. The questions and answers in this book will help you become more confident in the basics of investment alternatives, and which, if any, are appropriate in meeting specific goals.

This book is also meant to show you how questions can improve your money management know-how, and help you become a comparison shopper. You can become a "questioning detective" and uncover the clues you need to make the best decisions, save you money, and get you the best possible return for investment dollars.

LEARN TO PROTECT YOURSELF

Successful investment brokers and financial planners must be well trained in two important aspects of their industry: they must be extremely knowledgeable about the various products they can offer you, and *they must know how to sell*. The more investments you make for yourself, your family, and your future, the more money the investment professional makes.

I don't mean to say that every broker is only out for him or herself, or that brokers don't care about their clients. I do mean that in order for you to get the most out of your relationship with your broker, and to make the best, and most appropriate investment you can afford, you must do more than simply rely on an broker's advice. In order to do that, you need to be an "informed consumer" about investment options and about your particular needs and desires.

The problem is that the financial services industry is so complicated, and you're constantly being bombarded with new information. And when you find yourself in a face-to-face situation where you need specific—and vitally important—information, all the facts, figures, advice and opinions you've heard before fly right out the window. What can you do? How can you find out, right then and there, what you need to know?

You can ask questions.

There are only two ways to get information. One is by watching and reading. The other is by asking questions. You might get some clues about a broker by observing his behavior and personality. You can probably read up on investments and how they pertain to your situation. This is fine for preparation and background information, but the only way to get immediate information, direct from the source's mouth, and directly applicable to your own circumstance, is by asking questions.

WHY DON'T WE ASK MORE?

The reason we don't ask more questions is largely because we're afraid to question authority. We follow the tradition that says, "the financial professional knows more than I do." We're afraid to doubt his or her advice.

We're reluctant to ask questions because:

- We are afraid we'll be thought stupid if we ask too many questions.
- We assume that brokers know more than we do, therefore we have no right to ask questions.
- We assume that a persuasive broker is a competent broker.

- •We think we can never make reliable investment decisions alone, and don't want to alienate the broker.
- •We think because we're not making a large investment we shouldn't take up so much time or expect so much attention.

Brokers are commissioned salespeople. They are often hired and fired because of their sales ability. Your interests and the broker's may not be the same (i.e., products brokers recommend are often based on the amount of commission involved—not necessarily what's best for your portfolio). This is not to say that all brokers are only out for what they can get—but it is up to you to make the distinction and select a broker who wants to make money by helping you make yours.

Good agents have been trained as questioners themselves (unlike some salespeople who have been trained to make a pitch and keep talking until they close the sale). A simple way to tell a good broker is to open the conversation by asking "What would you recommend?" If the broker tries to convince you to make a particular investment without asking you any questions, you should be leery.

Brokers know the power of questions, and are often questioning experts. This book will provide you with the tools that will enable you to become a questioning expert yourself and get the information you need.

BUT WHAT DO I ASK?

Many times we don't ask questions because we're not sure what we should be asking. We assume these people are the experts, they know what they're talking about. "I don't know enough to make this decision myself. My broker is the one who knows all about investments—and besides, *I don't even know what questions to ask.*"

We are faced with difficult decisions every time we seek out financial advice, and often we come away with lingering doubts. "Was there something else I should have asked?" is the haunting refrain most of us have experienced after talking to a broker or financial planner.

You might wish you had an expert with you to get the necessary information. Well, now you have. This book will turn you into the expert. Take it with you when you see your broker. Or write down the pertinent questions that apply to your situation. For example, if you're interested in buying stocks, concentrate on the section about stocks; if you're thinking about retirement funds, turn to the sections on qualified pension plans and annuities.

Some of the questions are for you to ask yourself (for instance, before you consider making any investment, you may have to ask yourself if you prefer a conservative approach, or one with more risk but greater growth potential). Some questions are presented for your general knowledge about investments and help you define terms and concepts. The bulk of the questions are for you to ask your broker.

In writing this book, we set out to explore some of the key issues that are on people's minds. We tried to cover as many areas of investment as we could. There's no way we could address everyone's individual investment needs, but we tried to include the most important, and frequently asked questions.

Every question opens up other questions. Add your own questions to the list. We don't presume to have covered every possible investment situation. But the questions here should get you started, and should stimulate your own questioning process so that you, too, can get the information you really need.

WHY YOU NEED THIS BOOK
The purpose of this book is threefold:
1. To provide you with the questions to ask in order to get the information you need;
2. To get you into the habit of asking questions; and
3. To build your confidence in dealing with your broker.

After all, the person who asks the questions sets the direction and the topic in a discussion, and gains a sense of control in a difficult situation. Most psychologists agree that anxiety arises from loss of control. When you ask a question, the other person feels compelled to answer, and the power goes to the asker. (Just watch the power shift when someone asks you, "Where are you going?" and you answer, "Why do you ask?")

You don't have to take a broker's word for something just because she's a broker, or nod and say yes if you don't understand. You don't have to leave the office or get off the phone until you get a satisfactory answer, no matter how intimidating or aggressive the broker may seem. You have the right to ask questions, and the right to get answers. If a broker won't answer your questions, get someone who will. If a broker says she doesn't have time for explanations, there are other financial experts around who are willing and able to do so.

SOME VERY WILLING FINANCIAL EXPERTS
I was very fortunate, in writing this book, to have

found two experts who were not only willing and able to answer questions, but to ask them as well.

Joan P. Orazio, president of Orazio Financial Services, Suffern, New York, is a certified financial planner, a licensed NASD principal and representative and a licensed insurance broker. She has practiced financial and estate planning since 1975 and is widely recognized as an expert in personal planning for individuals, and employee benefit planning for small businesses and corporations. She is a well-known speaker and instructor on a variety of financial topics, and she has been written about and quoted in *Money*, *Barron's*, *USA Today*, and other noteworthy publications.

Lawrence B. Greenbaum started his career in real estate on Long Island, New York, until he found his calling in the stock market. He is currently a senior portfolio manager at a New York City investment banking firm where he specializes in equity securities, primarily growth stocks. Much of his investment philosophy he admits came from his father, a now-retired investor.

Joan, Larry, and I don't claim to have exhausted all the questions you could, or should, ask about investments. Nor do we intend to give you specific advice pertaining to your individual circumstances. We have provided questions and examples to give you a basis for comparison: we didn't want to simply provide you with a list of questions, and let it go at that. We wanted you to understand why each of the questions is important, and what you should expect to learn from your broker's answer. When you ask a question, you may want to compare your broker's answer to the one in the book.

THE HE/SHE ISSUE
One last word on a technical issue. We did not want to

include any gender bias in this book by constantly using "he" to refer to the broker. On the other hand, it is very awkward to use "he/she" and "him or her" throughout. So when referring to "the broker," we use "he" in some examples, and "she" in others.

AND FINALLY . . .

This is your opportunity to create a new relationship with your broker, and with your prerogatives as an informed consumer. Be an active participant in the most important areas of your life. Brokers are there to help you make some of the most important decisions for yourself and your family, and you have the right to a clear and comprehensive understanding of everything that affects you. Make sure you stand up for that right, and start asking smart questions.

SECTION 1

SMART QUESTIONS TO ASK ABOUT GETTING STARTED

There are questions you must ask yourself before you begin any investment program: questions about the current state of your finances; questions about how you see yourself and your family living in the years ahead; questions about what type of person you really are and how much risk you are willing to take.

It is important to take a hard look at where you are now in life, and what it is you are trying to accomplish, and then to set goals—short term, intermediate, and long term.

Whatever your goals are, the time to start thinking about making investments is NOW. However, it is important to remember "first things first." You can't begin to make investments if you can't pay the rent or feed your children. But you may be able to start on a small scale, putting away only a few dollars a week, so that you know you are working toward an important goal—taking care of your future.

You have to add yourself into your monthly budget. Think of yourself as a bill that must be paid, once the most basic necessities have been taken care of. It is never too early or too late to start, and your attitude can make a big difference. Don't think of investing as something only the rich can afford. Start asking questions before you think you have "enough" money to make investments, and you may find out about affordable options you knew nothing about. Or you may make a particular investment option a goal, learn all you can about it now, and then when you do have the money, you'll have the advantage of being an educated investor.

These are some of the questions you should be asking when you are considering an investment program:

WHERE AM I IN MY LIFE CYCLE?

This is an important question to ask yourself before you even think about investing. How much money you use for investment purposes, and how you invest that money should be directly related to where you are in your life cycle, in terms of your career, financial and personal goals:

1. Are you just starting out in your career?
This may mean your first full-time job, and your first opportunity to participate in savings programs. For example, unless it is a very small company, most

firms have payroll deduction plans, which allow for investment in savings bonds. Or the company may have a Credit Union, which will allow you to deposit money directly from your salary check, and in some cases, allow you loan privileges as well. Your company may also offer you participation in retirement savings plans.

Any opportunity for payroll deduction is usually a good time to start saving. Since the money is taken right out of your paycheck, you tend not to miss it, and accumulating savings is practically painless.

If your company does not offer any of these plans, or if you are self-employed, you should still investigate ways of starting an investment program, even if it's with as little as $50 a month (all of these programs will be discussed in depth in later sections of the book).

2. Are you in your thirties or forties?

As you get older, the emphasis tends to shift to accumulating funds for a home, whether it be a coop, a condo, or a single-family residence. Again, payroll deduction plans can be very useful, particularly because there are some which offer loan programs to employees.

At this stage, you'll probably want to make investments for your children's education or for your future retirement; you should begin to look into annuities and/or life insurance (discussed in Section 4).

3. Are you in your fifties?

Most people in their fifties are past the initial stages of purchasing homes and educating their children, and the focus shifts more heavily toward retirement. As the children leave home, there may be an increase in cash flow available for investment purposes. However, you may also be at your peak earnings stage now, and need to carefully consider your tax situation. Payroll deduction pension plans, and annuities which permit investment in mutual funds may be your best bet.

At this stage, it may be appropriate to begin thinking in terms of life after retirement, and whether you might need a supplemental income, either through a small home-based business or consulting work.

4. Are you in your sixites?

When retirement becomes more of a reality, income produced by investments can become a vital source of supplemental funds. Therefore, this is the time to be reviewing all your investments to determine just how much investment income you'll be receiving when you retire, and to make any necessary decisions regarding those investments.

If you've been investing wisely all along, you should have sufficient earnings to continue making some investments until age 75. Since life expectancy is getting longer, investment funds should be designed to continue earning you money until at least age 90.

WHAT IS MY INVESTMENT RISK TOLERANCE?

What is a good investment decision for one person isn't necessarily a good decision for another. Knowing yourself and how you relate to money is an important part of your investment success. Answer the following questions on a scale of 1–3:

- disagree = 1 point
- agree to some extent = 2 points
- strongly agree = 3 points

1. The most important rule is: never lose your capital. _____
2. Money invested in banks and government bonds will never do as well as money invested in stocks. _____
3. I don't mind the fact that I don't have ready access to my money if I can earn more in the long run. _____
4. I can accept the fact that my invested dollars may be worth more or less at any particular point in time if it gives me the opportunity to earn more money in the long run. _____
5. I will accept less money now to get more total return on my investment over a longer period of time. _____
6. I will accept a lower current yield so I can get my money back at any time. _____
7. I will accept less interest if I can have the assurance of government guarantees or insurance on bonds. _____
8. I am willing to place some money in lower-rated investments if they are professionally managed and I can receive a higher interest. _____

- Minimum risk tolerance 8–12 points
  You would be best off investing in products that offer

the most security, even though they may not offer the largest return. You might look into bank and U.S. Treasury Money Markets (see Section 3), Certificates of Deposit (see Section 3), or Fixed Deferred Annuities (see Section 4). You could be a little more aggressive, and invest in mutual funds (see Section 3), Variable Annuities (see Section 4), and the highest rated stocks and bonds.

- •Low risk tolerance   13–17 points
  You are a bit more of a risk-taker, and you might want to look into the more aggressive growth and income mutual funds, or to low capitalization stocks (see Section 3).

- •High risk tolerance   18–24 points
  You are willing to take higher risks to get higher returns. That should mean that you have more "disposable" money available to you. You might be interested in investing in property through Real Estate Investment Trusts (see Section 5), Limited Partnerships, and further diversification into Cable TV, Equipment Leasing, Oil and Gas, and Venture Capital.

WHEN IS THE BEST TIME TO INVEST?

The best time to invest is now. If you have a goal or objective you are trying to achieve, start investing in whatever small way you can, whenever you have the money.

Obviously it is wise to consider depressed "bear" markets as being the best times to invest, because prices are down, and "raging" bull markets as not being the right time because prices are high. However, as has been proven over and over, the best time is whenever you have money you don't need for essential services and can put away for future use.

HOW MUCH MONEY, OR HOW LITTLE, DO I NEED TO START INVESTING?

Most banks will accept a deposit of almost any amount to open a regular savings account, although some insist on a minimum of $100. Most mutual funds (see Section 3) have minimums of anywhere from $500 to $1,000. You can often open an IRA account (see Section 4) with as little as $50. Add-on investments, or additional deposits, can be made in any amount for bank accounts; most mutual funds do not accept sums less than $50. It doesn't take a lot of money to begin investing—the idea is just to GET STARTED!

SUPPOSE I WANT TO START INVESTING. CAN I HAVE EASY ACCESS TO MY MONEY WHEN I NEED IT?

There are two requirements for investments: one is money, the other is time. Initially, you need to have the money to invest. You also need to know that most investments take time to pay off. Everyone wants to "get rich quick," but most investments are designed to produce long-term results, not a fast buck. All investments, except money market and savings accounts, restrict your ability to get your money in a hurry without incurring penalties.

This means that some of your money should be invested with the idea that you will not be able to get it back without "paying a price" for it. Therefore, some of your money should be kept where you can get at it.

This "liquid" money should be in savings or money market accounts where money is readily available for withdrawal without any penalties. It may earn less interest there, but can be used as needed without any concern for market fluctuations or premature withdrawal penalties.

HOW MUCH LIQUIDITY SHOULD I HAVE?

The recommended amount of liquidity is enough to cover at least three months of running expenses; you may feel more comfortable with at least six months' worth of income readily accessible if needed.

HOW DO I DETERMINE HOW MUCH OF MY MONEY SHOULD BE PUT INTO IN THE VARIOUS KINDS OF INVESTMENTS AVAILABLE?

When making investment choices, it is most important for you to understand what you are trying to achieve. If your goal is to save money for a car, for example, you need to invest in something extremely safe and very liquid. You need to know that you can get your money out within a short period of time, and without incurring a penalty. You might use a regular bank savings account, a money market fund, or a short-term certificate of deposit.

On the other hand, if you are saving for your young child's education, or for your retirement, you want to make investments that will grow over a period of years and will give you the highest yields possible, even though you may

SMART QUESTIONS TO ASK ABOUT GETTING STARTED   19

not be able to withdraw that money until the investments mature without incurring a substantial penalty.

ARE THERE OTHER FACTORS TO CONSIDER?

You must decide what kinds of investments you would be comfortable making. Use your risk tolerance score to determine your investment personality. It won't pay for you to invest in a high-yield, high-risk product if that kind of investment is going to cause you a great deal of anxiety.

Also, you must take the time to look at the long-term (meaning ten years or more) performance of any particular investment instrument. For example, if you are looking at an aggressive growth fund for the education of your child, then you should look at the ten-year track record for this particular fund (see Section 3).

HOW DO I KNOW THE INCOME THAT I AM DRAWING FROM MY PRESENT INVESTMENTS WILL CONTINUE INTO THE FUTURE?

This depends on the type of investments you make. Stable income is possible with bonds and certificates of deposit to a greater degree than with any kind of mutual fund or stock. A certificate of deposit or bond that you purchase with a particular interest rate guarantees you will receive that interest to the maturity date.

On the other hand, a dividend-yielding fund and stock can either increase or decrease its dividend at any time. A mutual bond fund can lower or raise its monthly income per share depending on current interest rates. In other words, where no stated interest rate to maturity date exists, there is *no* guarantee.

So you must decide which type of investment is best for you: the type that guarantees a specific income (although small), or one that fluctuates, but offers the possibility of higher returns.

I AM WORRIED ABOUT FUTURE BUYING POWER, ESPECIALLY WHEN I STOP WORKING AND AM ON A FIXED INCOME. CAN SMART INVESTING HELP?

With the economy the way it is today, everyone should be worried about future buying power. Money is only as good as what it pays for. Our 1981 dollar now buys 56 cents' worth of groceries and gas for the car. If you want to protect and maintain your current life-style, you should be making investments which will give you income when you are no longer actively earning. A properly balanced investment portfolio can give you more of your money to keep.

Any investment that can be made pretax, such as the various contributory retirement plans (discussed in Section 4), can help a great deal. Money that would normally go to taxes can grow until retirement. After-tax or savings investments that can earn without current taxation also have a better chance to match your future retirement income needs. Remember—taxes and inflation erode your investment dollars, so you must keep both of these things in mind (and ask questions about the effects of your investment on both of them) when you make any investment decisions.

WHAT IS THE BEST WAY TO USE INVESTMENTS TO KEEP UP WITH INFLATION?

In order to keep up with inflation, your investment portfolio should balance interest-bearing investments with those that provide some promise of capital growth (the growth of the underlying principal).

For example, every portfolio should contain interest-bearing money markets, in which your funds are always available to you; bonds or bond funds which produce a steady income stream; and stocks or stock funds which provide capital growth.

It is capital growth that will keep you ahead of inflation. Your money lent to others produces interest. Capital presumes ownership and equity. Your money invested in stock or real estate grows with the economy and this "inflates" in inflationary times and protects your buying power.

HOW DO I KNOW THAT MY PRINCIPAL IS SAFE?

Many investments, such as those in banks, are covered by insurance. There are many bonds that are covered by governmental agency protection or insurance. That does not mean, however, that the price you can get when you sell any particular "safe" investment doesn't fluctuate with the market.

For instance, a Treasury Bond can be considered a safe investment, since it is guaranteed by the full faith and credit of the United States Government. However, investing your money in a 30-year Treasury Bond does not mean that it will be worth its full value at any point between when you buy it and its maturity date.

Suppose you purchased a 30-year Treasury Bond yielding 8 percent in the 1970s; if you wanted to sell it during the high-interest rate period of 1980–82, it would not have brought you more than 65 cents on the dollar. On the other hand, if you bought a 30-year Treasury Bond in the early years of the 1980s when the interest rate was 12 percent, and wanted to sell it when rates had fallen to 8 percent, you could receive much more than your initial investment. That means that even a very "safe" investment will go up and down in value relative to interest rates.

CAN I BORROW MONEY USING MY INVESTMENTS AS COLLATERAL?

Yes, you can. Collateralizing an investment portfolio is easier, however, if the portfolio contains high grade and readily salable investments, such as government or big corporation bonds and mutual funds.

HOW MUCH MONEY DO I NEED TO INVEST TO ENSURE THAT MY RETIREMENT YEARS ARE TAKEN CARE OF?

There is no universal answer to this question. It depends on your life-style, and where you live. There are retired people who can't live on $60,000 a year, and others who can get along fine on $20,000. You have to ask yourself questions about what you want out of life, and what's important to you. Do you want to travel? Do you want to sell your house and invest that money, or do you want to stay in the house? Do you want to relax and take it easy when you retire, or do you want to live it up and do things you never had time to do before? Each individual will have a different answer to each of those questions, so each individual must determine how much money should be invested to reach his or her goals.

It is important not to give up today for tomorrow. Some people do nothing but invest and save all their lives, and then don't live to enjoy their investments. Remember, the whole purpose of investing is to provide you with a happier, easier life.

SECTION 2

SMART QUESTIONS TO ASK WHEN CHOOSING A STOCKBROKER

An investment broker is your consultant and advisor. He helps you to clarify your needs and helps you to satisfy them by choosing the proper investments.

One of the most important questions you must ask before you shop for a broker is this: How can I choose a broker who will truly represent me and not be primarily concerned with how much commission he makes?

Ask your friends, neighbors, and relatives for references. Ask questions about how comfortable they are with their present broker, what kind of service they get, what problems they have encountered, and how professional the brokerage firm is.

A broker should be accessible, return your calls

24

promptly, answer all your questions, make suggestions, act professionally, and be able to handle your specific needs.

Good brokers will try to put themselves in your position and present to you the solutions they would consider if they were you. They should give you options to consider now, and in the future. They should not be suggesting investment options you cannot afford, or trying to convince you to take risks you are not willing to take.

Some considerations might be: Does the broker cut you off in midsentence, or does she let you finish your thought before responding? Does the broker take other telephone calls while in a meeting with you, or does he devote complete attention to you? Does the broker have set answers for each problem you explain, or does he offer several options for you to choose? Does the broker try to dominate the relationship, or does she let you have some input? Often a "gut" reaction about a broker is correct; if he or she seems to be too busy to focus on your problems, maybe this is not the broker for you.

The only way you can find out if a broker is right for you is by asking questions. You may not choose to ask the broker all of the questions in this section. But you do want to ask enough questions to get the information you need. You also want to find out how willing this broker is to answer any questions you might have, and how you react to this broker's manner and attitudes.

A good broker wants to be sure you understand what you're getting, and how much it will cost. If the broker is reluctant to answer any of your questions, find another broker. Choosing a stockbroker, like choosing a doctor, a lawyer, or any other professional, is a very important decision; if a broker does not understand your need to ask questions, then perhaps you should look somewhere else.

WHAT EXACTLY ARE THE LICENSING REQUIREMENTS FOR BROKERS?

In order to execute orders given to him by an investor, a broker must have at least minimum registration with the National Association of Securities Dealers (NASD). That means he must have successfully passed the investment company products/variable contracts exam (known as Series 6), or the General Securities Examination (known as Series 7).

A broker must be licensed in the state in which his office is located. He must be licensed in the state in which his client resides. Any broker selling an insurance product must be licensed by the insurance commissioner in the state where his office is located, and in any state where an insurance application is signed regardless of where the client signing the application resides.

All brokers, and the firms with whom they are registered, must adhere and be subject to the Federal Securities Laws and Rules of the stock exchange, the NASD, and the securities laws of the various states. As a registered representative of NASD, brokers have a professional obligation to conduct business affairs in a moral, ethical, and legal manner. They must be familiar with, and comply with, all laws, rules, and regulations of the securities industries.

IS THERE A NATIONAL LICENSING EXAM?

There is a national examination, given by the NASD. Each state has its own licensing requirements as well. To obtain a license, a broker must be sponsored by a retail brokerage house. The licensing exams are quite extensive, and require prospective brokers to know intricate details about stocks, bonds, mutual funds, the securities acts, and various other existing regulations.

The exams also test how prospective brokers would determine which types of investments are appropriate for individual clients. For example, the exam might include a multiple choice question like, "Suppose you have a client who is retiring and is interested in obtaining an income from investment. What would you recommend? (a) A Mutual Fund of Government Securities; (b) Options; (c) A stock fund; (d) Limited Partnership." In this case, (a) would be the correct answer.

DOES IT MAKE ANY DIFFERENCE IF MY BROKER WAS SPONSORED BY A LARGE BROKERAGE HOUSE, LIKE MERRILL LYNCH OR MORGAN STANLEY, OR BY A SMALLER HOUSE?

Larger brokerage houses often have excellent training programs. However, there is no guarantee that a broker from a large firm is a better broker. Many of the smaller "boutique" type houses produce some highly skilled professionals.

WHAT CAN I EXPECT MY BROKER TO DO FOR ME?

A broker should abide by the rule "know your client." That means that a broker's primary function is to help the investor select an appropriate investment based on goals and temperament, as well as the income, assets, and tax bracket of the individual investor.

WHAT SHOULDN'T A BROKER DO?

A broker should not accept orders from a third party for a customer's account without prior written authorization from that customer. A broker should never guarantee the present or future value or price of any security, or that any issuer of an investment will meet its promise of obligations. Brokers are not permitted to lend or borrow from a customer or make payment with their own funds for transactions by a customer. No broker should give tax or annuity advice to a customer unless they are qualified to do so by background or training.

HOW DO I GO ABOUT FINDING THE RIGHT BROKER FOR ME?

Personal recommendation by someone whose judgment you respect is the best place to start. Take the time to meet the broker and explain what you are trying to accomplish with your investment dollars.

SHOULD I INTERVIEW THE BROKER?

By all means. Finding a broker with whom you feel comfortable is as important as finding the right investment. You should ask questions such as:

WHY DID YOU CHOOSE THIS FIRM TO WORK WITH?

What you want to hear is that the broker did her homework in defining, and embracing, the respectability and code of ethics adhered to by the firm by which she is employed.

HOW LONG HAVE YOU BEEN WITH THIS FIRM?

This would indicate the amount of experience in the particular company, and might give you some indication of her satisfaction with the company and whether or not she intends to stay there.

WHAT IS YOUR EDUCATIONAL AND PROFESSIONAL BACKGROUND?

This would tell you her degrees, licenses, professional qualifications, and on-the-job training. Sometimes the best broker is the one who has had a broad educational background. Look for someone who will meet your needs. You want to be sure that if you are interested in options, for example, you are dealing with someone who has experience in that area of investment.

DO YOU SPECIALIZE IN ANY PARTICULAR INVESTMENT AREA?

It would be interesting and pertinent to know whether or not a broker is biased toward any particular investment area. There are some who feel very comfortable with stocks and bonds and do not feel comfortable dealing with insurance products. Others may deal almost exclusively with insurance products, and do not feel as comfortable with stocks. If you think you might be more inclined toward investing in a particular area, you would be better off finding a broker with experience in that field.

ARE THERE ANY LAWSUITS OR LITIGATION PENDING AGAINST YOU OR YOUR FIRM?

It is a measure of the prudent behavior of the firm as to how many suits they might have pending against them, or any arbitration hearings in which they have been involved. One of the first steps you can take to check out a financial advisor is to call your state securities department. Local numbers are made available by the North American Securities Administrators Association (NASAA) in Washington, D.C. (202-737-0900). When you reach your state securities department, someone there can enter the name of the individual or firm into a 50-state computer data bank, which is maintained by both NASAA and NASD to keep track of registered agents in any state.

The securities department will also have vital information on the broker's education, former employment, and whether or not he has ever filed for bankruptcy or been the subject of complaints. The department will also advise you whether the broker has any convictions for investment-related misdemeanors or infractions.

HOW CAN I BE SURE THAT THE SERVICE I AM RECEIVING IS FROM SOMEONE REPUTABLE?

You can only transact business on the stock exchange

if you are either a member yourself, or an employee of a stock exchange member. Employees of stock exchange member firms are required to pass proficiency tests and sign an agreement to follow certain standards of conduct if they deal with the public. Trade associations, most notably the NASD, have been particularly effective in establishing codes for guidance of firms and their employees.

The Federal Securities Acts were also passed to give the Securities and Exchange Commission far-reaching regulatory power. Most states have their own securities laws as well, which are called "blue sky" laws.

WHAT SHOULD I EXPECT MY BROKER TO ASK ABOUT ME? WHAT DOES HE NEED TO KNOW?

When you open an account with a broker or brokerage house, you will be asked to fill out a form with information about your finances. You will be asked to state all of your assets, including your gross income and your tax bracket. You'll also be asked to state your current liquidity—how much money you have that can be converted to cash in five days (such as savings accounts, stocks and bonds, as opposed to real estate which cannot be readily converted to cash).

WHAT ARE SOME OF THE SIGNS THAT THE BROKER REALLY CARES ABOUT ME AND IS JUST NOT INTERESTED IN OPENING UP A MASS ACCOUNT?

One sign is the time that the broker spends asking questions and trying to find out about you before any investment is made. For example, a broker should ask you about your investment goals. Is the investment intended for education or retirement? Is it needed in 5 years or 20 years? Do you need an income from this investment?

These kinds of probing questions can help you understand if the broker really wants to do the best for you.

HOW CAN I TELL IF MY BROKER IS REALLY LISTENING OR PAYING ATTENTION TO ME?

You have to listen to the broker and to the way in which she responds to your questions. Are her responses pat answers, or is she tuned in to your needs and desires? After meeting and speaking with her, ask her how she would characterize your investment personality. Ask her how she would describe your investment goals. Listen to her answers and see how well they match up with your own thinking in these areas.

SOME PEOPLE FEEL THAT THE BEST WAY TO CHOOSE A BROKER IS BY HOW SUCCESSFUL THAT PERSON HAS BEEN WITH HIS OR HER OWN INVESTMENTS. IS THIS THE RIGHT KIND OF CRITERIA TO USE IN SELECTING A BROKER?

A broker is successful if he does well by successfully investing other people's money—which you can only find out by getting references from other people who deal with that particular broker. Just because a broker looks successful doesn't necessarily mean he is a good broker. The fact that he owns a Rolls Royce or a Rolex may mean he's done well for himself, but it doesn't always mean that he has done well for his investors. You should be less impressed with the kind of car that someone drives than with a personal recommendation from someone you know.

SUPPOSE I DO KNOW SOMEONE WHO HAS WORKED WITH THIS BROKER. WHAT SHOULD I ASK HIM?

The most important factor is the kind of relationship this person feels he has with the broker. Is he comfortable about asking what might be considered a "stupid" question? Is the broker himself readily available to answer any questions? Is the broker only interested in talking to the client when an order is to be executed, or will he chat about other items of financial interest to the client—for example, can he ask his broker about his early retirement proposal, or whether or not he should lease a car? Does the broker suggest other financial professionals if he himself does not know the answer?

WHAT IF I DON'T KNOW ANYONE WHO'S USED THIS BROKER? CAN I ASK THE BROKER TO SUPPLY REFERENCES?

You can and you should. It is rare that a broker (or anyone else, for that matter) will send you to someone who is unhappy with his or her services. But in most cases in the brokerage business, clients will not agree to act as a reference unless they feel really strongly about that particular broker.

HOW DO BROKERS GET CLIENTS?

Many brokers get referrals from existing clients. However, most brokers get clients from cold calling. Brokers purchase lists of qualified investors from various marketing services. These lists might include subscribers to the *Wall Street Journal*, owners of sole proprietorships, etc. Many thousands of phone calls and long hours of prospecting go into building a solid client base.

I'VE HEARD ABOUT SCAMS INVOLVING BROKERS WHO CALL YOU ON THE PHONE TO TRY TO GET YOU TO INVEST IN SHADY DEALS. IS THIS SOMETHING I SHOULD LOOK OUT FOR?

There are always some bad apples in any industry, and some "boiler room" scams in the financial industry, but cold calling is a legitimate way of doing business and essential to the brokerage industry. However, sometime you may get a call from a stranger trying to sell you a "great deal" on oil in Texas or soybeans in Illinois. The caller doesn't know anything about you, except whatever information he or she was able to glean from the cold-calling list.

Brokerage houses used to use these lists to train younger people. As Joan Orazio tells it, "When I first came into this profession, it was quite common to use the 'smile and dial' approach. Most brokerage firms demanded that brokers make at least fifty phone calls a day." If a broker calls you, and the deal sounds too good to be true, it probably is. If it sounds like a legitimate deal, be sure you ask to meet with the broker, find out about the firm he represents, and do some of your own research about the stock he's offering.

HOW LONG SHOULD I STAY WITH A BROKER?

A broker should be judged on her performance. If you are making your own investment decisions, did the broker handle everything in a professional and timely fashion? Did she call you after your trades were executed? Was she available to answer your questions? Did she agree or disagree with your investment decisions that lost you money? Did she agree with decisions that made you money? As long as your broker is following your instructions, you really have no reason to change.

If you don't make your own investment decisions, but must rely on your broker for advice, then you must judge her on whether you made or lost money. Keep a record of your investor's suggestions, whether or not you follow them. That way you'll know that if out of six recommendations over the past year, five of them made money— even if you didn't invest in them—your broker is doing very well. If, on the other hand, five out of six were doing poorly, it may be time for a change.

You should constantly be evaluating your broker—but keep in mind that many investments take six months, a year, or longer before they start to pay off. Just because you don't see immediate results doesn't mean your broker is not doing a good job.

Be objective. If your broker gave you good advice which you disregarded, don't blame her. But if you didn't like her advice or her attitude, don't hesitate to change.

HOW DO I GO ABOUT CHANGING BROKERS?

If you have found a new broker you can open a new account with the new firm. Any cash and securities in your old broker's account can be easily transferred. Your new broker will send you a transfer form that you must sign and send back with a recent copy of your account statement from the original firm. Your new broker sends the transfer form to the original firm.

The transfer can take several weeks or longer. If you have cash in your old account, you may want to close your account, or remove the cash portion of your account, so that you can have use of that money right away. Most firms will send you a check against cash in the account immediately.

CAN I, AND SHOULD I, HAVE MORE THAN ONE BROKER?

This depends on the size of your portfolio (the dollar amount of your investments). Naturally, if you only invest a few thousand dollars in the market (or in bonds, etc.), one broker is adequate. If, however, you have millions of dollars to invest, you might want to give your business to several brokers. That way you will have more diversity, and if one broker is outperforming the others, then you might consider moving more of your assets to his firm.

There are thousands of stocks and investment ideas, and it's fair to say that it is difficult for any one broker to be an expert on all of the products available to investors today. So if you have a lot of money to invest, you may want to spread it out among several individuals with specific areas of expertise.

WHAT WILL IT COST ME TO DEAL WITH A BROKER?

This is not a simple question. Brokers make their money from commissions on sales. If you are talking about stock trades, then commissions will vary from one brokerage house to another based on the services performed or offered by that house. For example, a discount broker will offer no advice and will only execute trades. For that reason, they can employ people who simply execute orders and are paid on a straight salary. On the other hand, if you need the advice of a professional, and want to have questions answered about that particular trade or about any other transactions, then a full-service brokerage house will better serve your needs.

The scale of commissions for a full-service brokerage house is based primarily on the price per share and the number of shares in the transaction. That scale will vary from one full service broker to another. Both discount and full service brokers charge a minimum fee as well. Again, the fee will vary from one to another.

HOW CAN I HOLD TRANSACTION PRICES TO A MINIMUM?

If you are working with a broker you can trust, you'll probably be encouraged to participate in Direct Reinvestment Plans (DRIPs) offered by many of the corporations which trade stock. For example, AT&T will allow you to reinvest dividends and accept additional investments, at no additional charge, in order to encourage you to increase the number of shares in your account.

Any opportunity for direct investment through payroll deduction will also keep transaction fees at a minimum. Many companies have corporate stock purchase accounts which permit employees to purchase company stock at a discount, and with no brokerage fees.

WHAT KIND OF RELATIONSHIP DO I WANT TO HAVE WITH MY BROKER? HOW MUCH POWER AND AUTHORITY DO I WANT TO TURN OVER TO MY BROKER OR INVESTMENT PLANNER, AND HOW MUCH DO I WANT TO KEEP FOR MYSELF?

I recently met a very wealthy friend of my husband's, a multi-multimillionaire—and was astonished to find out that he doesn't know very much about his money! He's got a broker whom he trusts implicitly, and this broker makes all the investment decisions.

Turning over to someone else all the responsibility for your financial management is a very serious decision. What if the broker makes a choice that does not turn out well? Whom will you blame? What protection do you have?

If you give a broker total discretion over your funds, he will require you to sign a form that states that whatever decision your broker makes on your behalf, is, in effect, your decision. You will be turning over your ability to make financial decisions to someone else.

Many brokers and financial planners will not even accept discretionary accounts, because in today's litigious society, clients tend to sue if investment decisions do not pan out. Co-author Joan Orazio says investors are usually happier if they are actively involved in making investment choices.

WHAT IS A DISCOUNT BROKERAGE HOUSE, AND SHOULD I CONSIDER USING ONE?

A discount brokerage house is a firm which will accept and execute orders for clients. It does not render any advice, nor does it make any recommendations. If you can make your own decisions and do not need the research capability of a regular brokerage house, a discount house can work out well.

The real answer here is your ability and comfort level with making your own investment decisions. The discount broker is like a bank teller; she'll simply take your order and do what you ask her to do. You are, in effect, your own broker, and for this reason costs for investment transactions are considerably lower.

ARE THERE DIFFERENCES BETWEEN DISCOUNT BROKERAGE HOUSES?

The differences between discount brokerage houses are based primarily in the size of the operation. The smaller houses may have a higher commission schedule than a larger house even though they are both discount houses. The speed and manner in which transactions are reported back to you may also be related to the size of the operation, and the number and quality of their employees. That is why it is important to ask questions before you make any commitments—call several different houses and ask about their commission schedules, ask how transaction reports will be made, and find out who will be servicing your account.

WHAT ARE THE MAJOR DIFFERENCES BETWEEN REGULAR BROKERAGE FIRMS?

Again, size can be a factor, particularly concerning research and operations departments. In the past, larger firms had greater research capabilities and may have had more data available. Since the computer age, however, there really are no major differences other than those set by the management of each house as their primary objectives (for instance, some houses may specialize in mutual funds or municipal bonds). All companies try to be service oriented, some with greater success than others.

IF I'M THINKING OF CONNECTING WITH A PARTICULAR BROKERAGE HOUSE, SHOULD I READ ITS ANNUAL REPORT?

It's very difficult for the average person who does not read annual reports on a regular basis to get anything out of reading one. This report is put out by the company itself, and is usually a glitzy, expensive public-relations production. It's going to tell you what the company wants you to know, not what you may really need to know.

If you are interested in a particular company and want more information, there are research materials available in most public libraries, published by many research services such as Standard & Poor's and Value Line, which follow publicly traded securities of brokerage firms.

Smaller companies usually trade through larger houses. If you are dealing with a small company, it probably trades through a larger company. Ask your broker the name of the company through which his firm trades; then you can check out the larger company in the library.

WHAT SHOULD I BE LOOKING FOR WHEN I LOOK UP A COMPANY IN STANDARD & POOR'S? WHAT INFORMATION DOES IT CONTAIN?

A Standard & Poor's report will indicate the stock

exchange symbol for the company and the range of price for the entire year, its price-to-earnings ratio, its dividend, and its yield. It will show its Standard & Poor's ranking along with a summary of the company and its present position in the marketplace. You will also have data relating to the current outlook for share earnings, net earnings per share of common stock, and important company developments that have been researched by Standard & Poor's. It contains a lot of relevant information, particularly if there is any negative news on the horizon.

ARE MY ACCOUNTS COVERED BY INSURANCE?

All brokerage accounts are covered under the Securities Investor Protection Corporation (SIPC), which protects securities customers against a broker failure. Customers of a failed firm receive all securities registered in their names, and then receive, on a prorated basis, all remaining customer cash and the value of securities held by the firm. After that distribution, SIPC funds are available to satisfy the remaining claims of each customer account up to a maximum of $500,000. That sum includes a maximum of $100,000 on claims for cash. For example, if your total account is worth $500,000 but $200,000 is in cash, only $100,000 of the cash is insured by the SIPC. If, however, the cash is in a money market fund, it is considered a security and is totally covered.

Beyond that, insurance companies cover accounts from anywhere above that $500,000 up to as high as $10,000,000, depending on the firm involved.

Since there are variations from firm to firm, note the information provided on the forms the broker gives you for opening an account. Obviously, the larger amount of insurance is more important if you are going to have considerable sums per account.

WHAT IS THE SEC AND HOW DOES IT PROTECT ME?

The Securities and Exchange Commission monitors the sales, practices, and financial conditions of the industry very carefully. The SEC runs routine examinations of investment companies, and may become involved if there is a client complaint. Some authority may be delegated to industry self-regulatory agencies such as the New York Stock Exchange and the NASD. These agencies conduct thorough on-site investigations, examining files to be sure they include enough information about the clients, and that each file contains a client-signed agreement.

WHAT OTHER FINANCIAL PROFESSIONALS CAN HELP ME MAKE INVESTMENT DECISIONS?

An accountant can usually give you advice on the tax consequences of any investments you make or are considering. It is not uncommon for an insurance agent or attorney to offer advice as well, most frequently in the area of estate planning.

Your bank may be another source of professional advice. Most banks today offer a wide variety of services which may include financial planning, mutual funds, stocks and bonds, insurance and annuities. These are in addition to the usual bank offerings of money markets, certificates of deposit, safe-deposit boxes, etc. The key is to find someone who is not only professional, but knowledgeable and genuinely helpful.

In recent years, the certified financial planner has become important as a catalyst who can discuss goals and attitudes about money and translate information gathered into recommendations that address investment, insurance, taxation and estate planning needs.

HOW IS A CERTIFIED FINANCIAL PLANNER DIFFERENT FROM A BROKER?

From an investment point of view financial planners take the information you give them and work out recommendations in a written plan. If they are not licensed to implement the plan, you would go to another professional (a broker, an insurance agent, a lawyer—depending on your plan) for that.

On the other hand, there are certified financial planners who are also licensed insurance brokers, stock brokers, and have various other areas of expertise. Some may also be accountants or attorneys.

WHAT QUESTIONS SHOULD I ASK THE CERTIFIED FINANCIAL PLANNER TO FIND OUT HIS OR HER EXPERTISE?

You should ask a financial planner many of the same questions you would ask a broker about background, experience, and areas of specialty. One of the best questions to ask is how many of the planner's clients are similar to you in terms of age, occupation, size of assets, asset base, etc. You want to know that your planner has dealt with clients like you before because, although we are all unique, people in a given age group, given profession, or with a given asset base have many similarities in needs and objectives. The experience that planner has had in meeting those needs and objectives for others can be put to use for you as well.

HOW MUCH WILL ALL THIS ADVICE COST ME?

There are a wide range of charges, from no-charge consultations to very elaborate plans which can cost you thousands of dollars.

For example, some certified financial planners will meet with you at least once at no charge. There are some certified planners who charge a fee, ranging from $100 to $200 per hour, to create a personalized investment portfolio. If your situation is complex and includes areas such as investing for your children's education, investing for your retirement, and estate planning, the plan can be costly. Some planners offset any fees by collecting commissions generated by the investments you make.

DO ALL CERTIFIED FINANCIAL PLANNERS TAKE THE SAME EXAM?

There are actually six exams that deal with various areas of personal financial management. They are: cash flow management, risk management (meaning all areas of insurance), taxation management, investment management, estate management, and retirement planning. All are mandatory and are national exams, although these exams are now being redesigned, and will probably take a different form in the near future.

IS IT MORE ADVANTAGEOUS FOR ME TO GO TO A CERTIFIED FINANCIAL PLANNER WHO IS NOT A BROKER? WHO WOULD GIVE ME A MORE OBJECTIVE POINT OF VIEW?

You have to go to the person whom you trust and whom you feel will be objective. It is important to find the person you believe will work in your best interest. That is why you need to meet the individual broker or financial planner, and to feel that he understands your investment goals.

SECTION 3

SMART QUESTIONS TO ASK ABOUT THE SEVEN MOST COMMON TYPES OF INVESTMENTS

This section contains questions to ask about the seven most common type of investments people make: CDs, Money Markets, Stocks, Bonds, Mutual Funds, U.S. Treasuries, and Government Agency Obligations. The type of investment you choose depends on your specific goals and on your investment personality.

Many people start off making investments in CDs and money markets because they are well known, easy to purchase, and do not involve a lot of risk. They also do not give back a high rate of return. Money markets are attractive because they allow you unrestricted access to your funds; you can put money in and take it out whenever you want. CDs do restrict your ability to remove funds, but they have traditionally offered a safe investment vehicle with a moderate rate of return. Lately, however, interest rates on CDs have been falling, and you might do well to carefully examine other investment options.

When you start learning more about investment possibilities, you may be tempted to jump into the stock market. We all have fantasies of getting in on a good deal, and making a killing in the market. Remember, these are fantasies. Investing in the market requires a lot of time and study. Even the experts disagree constantly on which way the market will go, so there is no way to be sure that a stock you think a winner will turn out to be one.

You really should not consider investing in the stock market unless you have discretionary funds—money that you can *afford to lose*. Everyone loses in the stock market some of the time; small investors hoping for a quick return lose more often than most. That is why it is vitally important that you ask questions. The more you know, the better your chances for making smart choices.

If you're looking for a long-term investment that will provide you with income (interest payments), bonds may be a good choice for you. This is the type of investment that takes a long-range view, and is only appropriate if you don't have need of these funds for many years. If you sell or cash in your bonds before maturity, you stand to incur substantial penalties.

Many people like the idea of investing in our country, and are attracted to U.S. Treasuries and Government Agency Obligations. These investments can be complicated, however, and are not without risk. As with any investment, you must be sure you understand all your options and make choices based on facts, not emotional judgments. The best way to do that, of course, is by asking questions.

One of the easiest ways to get started as an investor is to purchase shares in a mutual fund. A mutual fund is a selection of professionally bought and managed stocks, bonds, money market investments, or combinations of these securities. Mutual funds permit you to pool your investment dollars with other individuals who have similar investment goals.

There are three distinct advantages to mutual funds. The first is diversification — a fund has a large and varied portfolio, so that if one type of investment in the fund is not doing well, another may be offsetting any losses. The second advantage is affordability. Most mutual funds have low minimum investment requirements. And the third advantage is professional management. All portfolios are handled by professionals whose job it is to manage the investments in accordance with the goals and objectives set forth in the prospectus for each fund. Although there are no guarantees that these goals will be achieved, you usually have a much better chance for success than if you were trying to "go it alone."

SMART QUESTIONS TO ASK ABOUT CDS

WHAT IS A CD?

A CD is a Certificate of Deposit, which is a contractual obligation of a bank to pay a stated rate of interest on a stated sum of money to maturity date. Because CDs (which may also be referred to as time deposits) are issued by banks, they are insured by the Federal Deposit Insurance Corporation (FDIC) or

Federal Savings and Loan Insurance Corporation (FSLIC).

IS THE STATED RATE OF INTEREST THE SAME AT ALL BANKS?

The maximum interest rates at which certificates of deposit may be issued are regulated by the Federal Reserve System. However, the interest rates actually offered vary from bank to bank. Rates are usually posted in the bank itself, and most banks will tell you over the phone the rates they are currently offering. Don't reject a bank with high rates just because it is not in your neighborhood. Many banks allow you to open CD accounts by mail. Therefore, it is in your best interest to shop around.

IS THE INTEREST TAXABLE?

Yes, the interest is taxable each year even if you don't withdraw it.

IF I NEED TO WITHDRAW MY MONEY BEFORE THE CD MATURES, WILL THERE BE A PENALTY?

This varies from bank to bank, but most do have a penalty for early withdrawal. It can be up to six months of interest and can include loss of principal as well. Make sure you ask the bank about penalties before you make the deposit.

CAN THE BANK REFUSE TO CASH IN MY CD EARLY?

Technically, the bank can refuse payment if it would hurt other depositors or the bank. For example, if a great many depositors wanted to cash in their certificates of deposit at one time and were to cause a "run on the bank," it could endanger the bank's day-to-day cash flow operation. In that situation, the bank could refuse to cash in your CD. Generally, this is not a problem although it does depend on the strength of the bank.

CAN THE BANK CASH IN MY CD EARLY WITHOUT MY CONSENT?

Yes, the bank can cash in your CD before maturity, and this has been happening more and more often in the last few years. In the case where a bank has been taken over by another bank, the new bank can restate the terms of the CD to current rates. There are usually no withdrawal penalties if you decide that you don't like the new terms and want to take your money elsewhere.

WHERE CAN I PURCHASE CDs?

CDs may be purchased directly through a bank or you can buy them through brokerage houses (these are known as brokered CDs). You can also get CDs through investment in some mutual fund companies.

ARE BROKERED CDs DIFFERED FROM CDs BOUGHT DIRECTLY THROUGH THE BANK?

They are basically the same instrument but they are traded at market value. This means that if you need your funds before the maturity date of your CD and don't want to incur an early withdrawal penalty, you could sell your CD through the brokerage house. The price you would get would be determined by: the current interest rate, the stated interest rate on your CD, and the amount of time left until maturity.

Because of the volume generated by brokerage houses, the rate or yield at purchase can be greater than that which is generally available by individual purchase. Most brokers sell CDs as an accommodation to their investors since the fees charged are minimal.

HOW SAFE ARE CDs?

Most CDs are either FDIC or FSLIC insured for accounts up to $100,000 (including interest). Check with your bank to make sure their CDs are covered under one of these agencies.

SMART QUESTIONS TO ASK ABOUT MONEY MARKETS

WHAT ARE MONEY MARKETS?

Money market accounts are not very different from regular savings accounts. They pay interest, provide safety of principal, and offer liquidity (meaning that your money is available to you whenever you want it). The difference is that banks invest money market funds in short-term, higher yielding instruments. Money market accounts are offered through banks and mutual funds.

Insurance companies which offer variable annuity contracts (see Section 4) may also make money markets available as one of their choices. However, these have more restrictions and do not offer the same liquidity and withdrawal ability as money markets purchased through banks and mutual funds.

WHAT KIND OF SECURITIES DO MONEY MARKETS INVEST IN?

Money market accounts are invested in very short-term bonds, generally no more than 90 days to maturity. Government money markets invest only in government securities. Tax-free money markets invest in municipal bonds. General money markets will invest in a combination of government securities, high-grade commercial paper (an extremely short-term corporate IOU, usually due in 270 days or less), CDs, and repurchase agreements.

HOW DO I KNOW WHERE MY MONEY MARKET IS INVESTING MY FUNDS?

Mutual fund and variable annuity money markets both offer a prospectus, or explanation, of their investment strategies containing descriptions of the kind and quality of investment instruments contained in their portfolios. All money market accounts in banks are insured, therefore the quality of investments is of less importance to the investor than mutual fund or variable annuity money markets.

IS THE INTEREST RATE FIXED?

No, the interest rate varies with the short-term bond

market and could change as often as daily. Interest may be simpled and figured on the average monthly balance or compounded daily and credited either monthly or whenever a transaction is made (e.g., deposit or withdrawal).

ARE MONEY MARKET ACCOUNTS A GOOD INVESTMENT FOR ME OR FOR MY BUSINESS?

These accounts offer liquidity without fluctuation of principal. Therefore, they are good for emergency funds and funds set aside for short-term goals (e.g., purchase of a house, car, etc.).

Since government money markets only invest in government securities, they have the added advantage of no state taxation on interest earned. They are certainly a valuable holding account for business as well as for individual investors.

IS A MONEY MARKET A BETTER INVESTMENT THAN A REGULAR SAVINGS ACCOUNT?

Money markets usually offer a higher current rate of interest than regular savings accounts. Inquire at various banks for their money market account rates and their regular savings account rates before you invest. (Be aware that banks sometimes use titles other than "money market" for these accounts such as "Super Saver" or "Priority Account." Ask which are the money market accounts.) However, in an environment when interest rates are declining, some of the regular savings accounts are yielding higher rates than money markets in the same bank.

ARE MONEY MARKET ACCOUNTS INSURED?

Bank money markets are insured by the FDIC up to $100,000 and are usually invested in government securities. Mutual fund money markets are as secure as the securities in which they invest. They can be invested 100 percent in government securities and be very secure. They can also be invested in a wide variety and quality of higher-yielding short-term municipal or corporate securities and be less secure.

Mutual fund money markets are usually valued at $1 per share. This makes them look the same as bank money markets. There have been occasions in the past few years when the value of shares would drop below $1 because of defaulted short-term securities, but the mutual fund managers added capital to make up the losses. There is, however, no guarantee that they will do that in the future.

If you want your funds totally liquid and available, check very carefully before you invest. Read the mutual fund money market's prospectus and be sure you understand where your money is being invested. Read the major financial publications such as *Money* and *Changing Times* for their reviews of the fund's performance. A good rule to follow is to stay with the biggest funds, since they have "deep pockets" and would be most able to cover any problems which might arise.

SMART QUESTIONS TO ASK ABOUT STOCKS

WHAT EXACTLY IS A STOCK?

A stock (also known as an equity security) is a share of ownership in a business, company, or corporation. This share entitles the holder to a percentage of all assets and earnings (proportionate to the number of shares owned), as well as voting rights.

For example, when you own a share of IBM you own a percentage of all the assets and earnings—and the liabilities—of IBM. As a stockholder, you are entitled to dividends if they are distributed, and you are entitled to voting rights. All stockowners own a piece of the company; the same voting rights exist for the holder of 1 share as for the holder of 1,000 shares (your percentage of votes changes according to how many shares you own, but your right to vote remains the same).

WHAT ARE MY VOTING RIGHTS AS A SHAREHOLDER?

All shareholders in a corporation, even if they only own one share, have the right to vote on all issues concerning the present or future of the corporation. This may include changes in policy, in accounting firms, in major philosophy, in pension plans, bonus packages, etc.

WHAT KIND OF STOCK MAY I PURCHASE?

You may purchase stock in a business, company, or corporation* which is publicly registered on a national and/or international exchange (such as the New York Stock Exchange, the Boston Stock Exchange, the American Stock Exchange, etc.).

---

*For simplicity's sake, these terms are used interchangeably throughout this section.

CAN I PURCHASE STOCKS IN A PRIVATELY HELD COMPANY?

Companies that are privately held do not offer stock for sale on any exchange. If the company does offer stock, it is done through the people who own the company. Many smaller businesses are set up as corporations with a very limited number of stockholders, usually family members or a combination of family and key personnel; however, some large corporations are privately held as well. One example of a well-known privately held company today is Levi Strauss.

WHY DO CORPORATIONS SELL STOCKS, OR "GO PUBLIC"?

Privately held corporations often go public because the original corporation, or the individual(s) who formed it, need more capital for the "growing" of the business than they can (or wish to) borrow from other sources such as banks. A good example of a privately held company which, after many years of operation, became a publicly held company is Reader's Digest. Until recently, Reader's Digest was held by a small group made up primarily of family members. After the death of the last family member, the stock was brought public.

WHAT IS THE NEW YORK STOCK EXCHANGE?

The New York Stock Exchange (NYSE), established in 1792, is located at 11 Wall Street in New York City. Stock trading is done on the floor of the exchange in person by brokers, traders, and specialists. Each stock is assigned only one specialist, who stands at an actual trading post. Brokers from firms, or traders for their own personal accounts, go to the post in order to execute buy and sell orders.

WHAT DOES IT MEAN TO HAVE A SEAT ON THE STOCK EXCHANGE?

Having a seat on the stock exchange entitles an individual and/or a brokerage firm to buy and sell securities on the floor of the exchange. Without a seat you cannot conduct business on the floor.

Seats can be bought, sold, or even leased. Prices have ranged from several hundred thousand dollars to well over one million dollars.

Large brokerage firms usually have a seat on the NYSE and are referred to as "member firms." These firms must adhere to all the rules of the NYSE. Smaller firms often have arrangements with member firms to execute their orders when necessary for a fee.

WHAT IS THE DOW JONES?

The Dow Jones is an index of major corporations. The Dow Jones Composite is 65 stocks broken down as follows:

    30 industrial stocks
    20 transportation stocks
    15 utilities stocks

The Dow Jones Industrial Average (the DJIA) is the most commonly referred-to average, and is a measure of economic strength and industrial production. Some of the corporations included in the DJIA are AT&T, Bethlehem Steel, Coca-Cola, General Motors, IBM, McDonald's, Proctor & Gamble, Union Carbide, and Westinghouse.

The DJIA is an advance indicator: the average responds to future economic conditions. For example, the stock market crash in 1987 occurred six months before we went into a major recession. In January 1992 the DJIA broke a record 3200, closing at an all-time high. This has led some analysts to believe that we are due for a strong recovery.

The transportation and utility averages measure those sectors of our economy. Some of the companies represented on the DJTA include Airborne Freight, Federal Express, Consolidated Rail, and Union Pacific. Utilities include Consolidated Edison, Detroit Edison, Pacific Gas & Electric, and Philadelphia Electric. Some analysts look to these three averages to determine the overall direction of the economy and the stock market in general.

Other indexes are the Standard & Poor's 500, consisting of 400 industrial stocks, 20 transportation stocks, 40 financial stocks, and 20 utilities stocks; the Willshire 5000, consisting of the broadest and largest number of the stocks, and the Value Line 1700.

WHAT DO THE TERMS BULL MARKET AND BEAR MARKET MEAN?

A bull market is one in which prices are on the rise and the Dow Jones Average is increasing. Generally, more buying than selling is taking place. Corporate earnings and profits are increasing, the economy is growing and, usually, interest rates are falling. Investors expect prices to rise.

A bear market is just the opposite. It is a market in which stock prices are declining, corporate profits are decreasing, and the economy is contracting or slowing down. Interest rates may be rising and quite high. More people are selling than are buying and the market is declining.

Since the market is always fluctuating up and down, it is only after weeks or months that a trend or direction can be established by charting the movement of stocks and the Dow Jones. Analysts often disagree as to whether we are in a bull or a bear market. A bullish investor is an optimist and will usually be buying more stocks in any market. A bearish investor, who sees the market as a pessimist, will sell his positions to protect against what he believes will be a declining market. These differing points of view are due to the fact that investing in stocks is not an exact science, and analyzing the market is open to many different interpretations.

HOW CAN I GO ABOUT BUYING STOCKS?

First you must open an account with a brokerage firm. When you want to buy a specific stock, you must place an order to purchase. Then you must tell your broker whether you want to pay market price or place a limit order (see below). When your broker makes a purchase for you, the order generates a confirmation of purchase, a bill which you must pay within five business days. You then become a stockholder.

WHAT IS THE DIFFERENCE BETWEEN MARKET PRICE AND A LIMIT ORDER?

If you place an order at the "market" price, you will pay the going price for that share when your order reaches the stock exchange floor. A "limit" order, however, tells your broker how much you are willing to pay for a specific stock. For example, you can instruct your bro-

ker to purchase 100 shares of a certain stock at $50 per
share, but no higher.

WHAT IS AN OPEN ORDER?

An open order is one that is based on a limited time
frame. It can be Good Till Canceled (GTC) or a Day Order
which is only good for the day on which it's ordered.

Suppose you want to buy 100 shares of IBM when the
price is $90 per share. If you place a Day Order, and the
price does not go down to $90 on that day, your order is
not carried out and the order is canceled.

If, however, that same order is put in as GTC, then it
will remain an open order at the brokerage house until
such time as a share of IBM is selling for $90. When that
happens, the order will be executed. Open orders are
usually posted on your monthly statement, and will be
automatically executed when the stock hits the named
price unless specifically canceled.

WHAT IS A STOP LOSS ORDER?

A stop loss order is usually used as a basis for selling a
stock once it reaches a certain price. Suppose you purchased a stock for $40 per share, and the stock's current
market price is $50 per share. If you wish to limit your down-
side risk, or any possibility for loss, you can put in an order
to sell if the stock goes down to $45 per share. That would
be a reduction from the current market price, but would still
give you a profit since you purchased the stock for $40.

A stop loss order cannot guarantee, however, that you
will get your $45 per share. It can only guarantee that if
the stock price drops to $45, your order for sale will be

"on line" and will be executed at the market price for that share when your order is received.

You can understand the reason for that if you look at the events of "Black Monday" in October 1987 when the market dropped 508 points in one day. There were many stop loss orders that day that fell far below the stop price before they were executed. Suppose, on the previous Friday, IBM closed at $135 per share. You could have put in a stop loss order at $120. However, because prices dropped so rapidly on Black Monday, by the time your order was received, the stock could have been going for $104. Therefore, it is conceivable that your order would have been executed at $104.

WHAT IS A COMMON STOCK?

Common stock entitles you to a share in the ownership of a corporation and all its net assets and earnings. Common stockholders bear all the risks of ownership and are the recipients of the rewards of success.

If the company is profitable, the stock can earn you money in two ways. The first is through *dividends*; the second is through *appreciation* (see below).

The downside is that in the event of a corporate bankruptcy, common stockholders are among the last to receive any compensation from the dissolution of the corporation.

WHAT ARE DIVIDENDS?

A dividend is a payment made to a stockholder of his or her share of the company's earnings. Dividends are usually paid quarterly; however, dividend payments vary from stock to stock. Dividends may be declared and paid, may increase periodically, or may be eliminated.

The paying of dividends is dependent upon the primary goal of the corporation. If growth is its primary goal, then funds generated as profit will be reinvested into the business, and will not be passed through to investors.

WHAT IS APPRECIATION?

When a company becomes more successful, the value of its stock usually goes up, and so does the value of your investment. That is known as appreciation.

WHAT IS PREFERRED STOCK?

Preferred stock is usually more expensive to purchase since it contains more benefits for the stockholder. Preferred stocks generally have a fixed dividend, which is good for you when times are bad, but may not be so good if the company is doing extremely well and your dividend is not increasing. However, the dividend can be cumulative, meaning that if there are no funds available for distribution, the obligation to pay would accrue until funds were available. Also, in the event of financial problems, preferred stockholders receive compensation due before common stockholders receive anything. Normally, preferred stockholders do not have voting rights, although there are exceptions to this rule.

WHAT IS A GROWTH STOCK?

Growth companies, by description, are those that reinvest most of their earnings into the development of the company, as opposed to distributing the earnings as dividends. An example would be a company whose earnings and sales are expanding at a faster rate than the general economy, and whose stock is rising in value faster than other stocks. Earnings are retained for further expansion of the company. There is, therefore, greater potential for increase in the value of each share. This is known as *capital appreciation*. Growth stocks can provide investors with a higher "total return."

WHAT DO YOU MEAN BY TOTAL RETURN?

Total return refers to the combination of income and increase in value that a stock can provide. The overall purpose of investment is to receive the best possible total return on capital. For example, if a stock is returning a dividend of 6 percent and the price of the stock itself goes from $50 to $55 in a year, there has been a total return of 16 percent—6 percent for the dividend and a 10 percent rise in the price per share (from $50 to $55).

WHAT DOES THE TERM "BLUE CHIP" STOCK MEAN?

The term blue chip refers to a blue casino chip—the blue chip is the most expensive chip and therefore the one you want to hold onto.

Blue Chip stocks are those considered to be high-grade investment quality issues of well-known, major companies with long track records of earnings and dividend payments in all kinds of economic cycles. Good examples of blue chip stocks are companies such as IBM, General Electric, and Proctor & Gamble.

WHAT ARE OVER-THE-COUNTER STOCKS?

OTC stocks tend to belong to smaller companies, and are not traded on the major stock exchanges. These stocks are bought and sold directly through dealers.

HOW ARE OTC STOCKS SOLD?

The over-the-counter market is a negotiated market that uses a telephone and a computer network to link dealers in order to transact business. Market makers (brokers or firms that own selected securities) post their prices for buying and selling their particular security on the computer network, known as National Association of Securities Dealers Automated Quotation System (NASDAQ).

There can be many market makers for the same security, all with different bids and offers. Firms looking to buy or sell securities for their clients can look on the NASDAQ to see who is offering (selling) the stock, or who is bidding (looking to buy). The brokerage firm's trader can then contact the market maker with the best price and execute the order for his broker's client.

WHAT IS A PENNY STOCK?

Penny stocks traditionally refer to stocks selling for $5 or less per share. These stocks are usually traded over-the-counter from "Pink Sheets" (lists of companies that actively market these securities), and are not traded on any exchange.

Penny stocks are generally issued by very small companies that are selling stock to raise capital for reinvestment into their businesses in an attempt to promote growth. Penny stocks can be very appealing to the small investor since they do not require large amounts of money to invest. However, although it is possible to do well with penny stocks, there is a great degree of risk involved. Most over-the-counter stocks do not survive long term, and in the past there have been many scams associated with penny stocks.

WHY SHOULD I BUY A STOCK? WHAT'S THE BENEFIT TO ME?

In most cases stock well purchased, meaning purchased at the right price, will deliver a much greater total return than any other investment you can make. For example, if you invest $10,000 in a CD that earns 6 percent, when it matures you will have your $10,000 plus the 6 percent ($600) it promised to pay you. However, you can put $10,000 into 1000 shares of stock which you purchase for $10 a share. Even though that stock may only pay $.03 a share in dividends, you can have greater total return if the stock price goes from $10 to $12 in a year. The net result would be a $2,000 profit in the shares plus $30 in dividends for a total value of $12,030.

However, because of the market cycles, you should not buy stock unless you are planning to hold it for a long period of time. If you are buying a stock at the high point in a cycle, you may have to wait for the stock prices to go down and then come back up again before you can make a profit. Nothing goes straight up in the stock market. But over time you'll probably do much better in the stock market than in the bond market or in the bank, in terms of total return.

IS INVESTING IN STOCKS FOR EVERYONE?

Everyone should invest for the future. Humans now have potential lifespan of 90 to 100 years; however, we usually only work for 40 or 50 of those years. Social Security does not pay you enough to survive when you stop working, and unless you know you're going to inherit a great deal of money, you must start your investment planning as early as possible.

Stocks should *not* be part of that investment planning if you have no other resources on which to draw. You must have adequate available resources to handle any emergency. Before you invest any money in stocks, you must have proper health care and disability coverage, particularly if you are a single person and dependent on your paycheck, if you are self-employed, or if you are older and living on a fixed income.

If you do not have funds available to cover you in emergency situations, you should not be investing what money you do have in the stock market.

IF I DECIDE TO INVEST IN STOCKS, WHAT'S THE BEST WAY TO GET INVOLVED?

This is a matter of personal choice, and depends on your investment personality. There are many different ways to purchase stocks. You can acquire individual stocks by purchasing shares in an individual company. You can buy a composite of stocks in many companies by purchasing mutual funds (discussed in detail later on in this section). You can buy stocks by sector, meaning you can buy shares in particular kinds of companies, such as health care or utilities. There's also a new category called social investment, where you invest only in companies whose policies are more in tune with social issues such as environment and human rights.

Whether you invest in individual companies or in a stock mutual fund, your dollars are considered to be "in the market." The only difference between the two methods is one of management. Individual stock ownership requires that you manage your own portfolio, whereas mutual funds have portfolio managers who decide what and when to buy and sell.

HOW LONG SHOULD I HOLD A STOCK?

In large measure this will depend on the reason you bought the stock in the first place, and on the stock's performance.

For example, suppose you recently purchased shares in ABC Inc., a company that has been growing for a number of years. Now, however, ABC is experiencing a decline in earnings, a change in management, or the company is sold and its direction changes. It might be a good idea to sell this stock, even though you have only owned it for a short time.

There are many brokers who advise that purchase and sale be timed to either the growth potential you expect or the loss you are willing to take. Suppose you paid $20 a share for your ABC stock. It is now at $40 per share, and you feel sure it won't go much higher. It's probably time for you to sell.

By contrast, it is sometimes wise to set a limit on the loss you are willing to accept in a particular issue. What if you paid $20 per share for your ABC stock and it declines to $15 per share? You might consider that a sufficient loss and not want to risk a further decline in capital value. This is an important time to ask your broker and/or financial advisor for professional advice.

IS THERE A WAY FOR ME TO INVEST ON A REGULAR BASIS?

Some companies in which you can buy stocks offer what is known as a Direct Reinvestment Plan (DRIP). This means that instead of sending out a dividend to you, the company will automatically invest your dividend into buying more shares. You need only buy one share of stock in order to become a shareholder in a corporation which provides a direct reinvestment plan. Ask your broker to tell you about companies that have such plans.

HOW DO I KNOW THE STOCK MY BROKER RECOMMENDS IS A GOOD STOCK?

It depends on the relationship you have with your broker. If you have faith in the broker, then you have to have faith that he's done his homework before he made the recommendation.

WHERE CAN I GET MORE INFORMATION ON THE STOCK MY BROKER IS RECOMMENDING, OR ON ANY STOCK WHICH INTERESTS ME?

If you are interested in a particular stock, call or write the company and ask for a copy of their annual report. Your broker may even have a copy, and your library may have copies of reports from larger corporations.

Libraries have other information sources as well. They subscribe to research reports such as those provided by Standard & Poor's and Value Line. *Standard & Poor's New York Stock Exchange Reports* is an excellent reference source. It contains information on each company listed with the NYSE, including a description of the company, its economic outlook, and a ten-year statistical history. There is also a booklet published monthly called *Standard & Poor's Stock Guide* which contains abbreviated information on over 5,000 stocks. For information on this guide and other S&P publications, write: Standard & Poor's Corp., 25 Broadway, New York, NY 10004, or call 212-208-8000.

Value Line Investment Survey is another important resource. It includes a ranking of stocks, an analysis of the current market conditions, and an in-depth study of one particular stock in each issue. For more information about their publications, write: Value Line, Inc., 711 Third Avenue, New York, NY 10017, or call 212-687-3965.

You may also want to read financial newspapers and magazines, including the *Wall Street Journal*, the *New York Times*, the *Chicago Tribune*, *Barron's*, *Money*, *Fortune*, *Forbes*, *Business Week*, and *Better Investing*.

WHAT KIND OF STOCKS ARE GOOD INVESTMENTS FOR AN "UNSOPHISTICATED" INVESTOR?

It is not a good idea for unsophisticated investors to put their money into individual stock market issues. If you are an unsophisticated investor, you would probably be much more comfortable with a mutual fund, which is, basically, a pool of investments into many different kinds of stocks. Managers select what companies to invest in and decide when to buy and when to sell individual issues. Your risk is lower, since there are many stocks in the pool, and while some stocks will undoubtedly go down, others will go up in value. Also, you don't have to make the choice of which stocks to buy; someone else, with more knowledge and resources, makes that decision for you.

A FRIEND OF MINE JUST TOLD ME ABOUT A HOT STOCK. WHAT SHOULD I DO?

Investing your hard-earned money in any stock without taking the time to do your own homework is no different from rolling the dice at Atlantic City. You are taking a chance. Most people who are turned off to stocks and stock investing have been "burned" in just this way. It is much more prudent to ask your friend for the background information on the company that is so "hot" before you decide to put your "cool money" into it.

I'VE HEARD MY BROKER RECOMMEND A STOCK FOR AN "UNDERVALUED" COMPANY. WHAT DOES THAT MEAN?

Usually it means that there is potential in the company which the price of its stock does not yet reflect. Do your own research, and find out if Wall Street analysts also consider the company undervalued.

Look at the stock price track record over the last few years. If the share price is at a particular market low, it could mean there are problems within the company, and the stock price is down with good reason.

Sometimes, however, the price of a stock can be driven below its value by outside circumstances. For example, the price per share of some excellent companies was pushed down when we were threatened with war in the Middle East, despite the fact that earnings and net profits were up for the particular company. When outside events influence the market, good, valued companies may have reduced stock prices. Sometimes rumors can drive a stock price up or down. If earnings reports indicate that earnings are less than were projected or if a dividend is cut and stock prices go down, an investor with vision and patience can profit from the temporary undervaluation.

CAN I SUE MY BROKER IF I LOSE MONEY ON A STOCK SHE RECOMMENDED?

If you think that the recommendation was "inappropriate," you may sue. A broker is trained to make appropriate investments for each investor based on the investor's age, assets, available funds, and stated goals. For example, suppose you are retired and you want to invest your $50,000 life savings. If, on your broker's recommendation, you invest all the money in a single growth stock and lose a large portion of your money, you would have the basis for a suit since that would be a very risky investment for someone in your circumstance.

The National Association of Securities Dealers receives complaints and can hold arbitration hearings. If a broker or brokerage house is proven to be at fault, they are responsible for settlement obligations and costs. Many brokerage houses carry liability insurance to protect them against such a situation.

WHAT IS A STOCK CERTIFICATE?

A stock certificate is a piece of paper that shows the name of the company, the state in which it is incorporated, amount of shares purchased and to whom the shares are assigned. Most certificates are held by the brokerage firm for the client in "street name." This means that the shares are under the name of the brokerage house. If the stock has been fully paid for, this certificate must be "segregated and separate," and held in the client's account.

WHAT IF I WANT TO KEEP THE STOCK CERTIFICATE MYSELF?

If you want to take physical possession of your stock certificate, you may ask your broker to "transfer and ship." Your broker will then send the certificate to a Registrar and Transfer Agent who will destroy the street name certificate and issue a new one in your name.

You then become responsible for the safekeeping of the stock certificate. Your best bet is to store such a certificate in a safe-deposit box or fireproof safe.

WHAT IF I WANT TO SELL MY STOCKS ONCE I HAVE TAKEN DELIVERY OF THE CERTIFICATE?

If you want to sell your stocks, you have to endorse the back of the certificate and send it back to your broker. However, since endorsing a certificate is like endorsing a check, you don't want to send a signed certificate through the mail for fear it might be lost or stolen. If you do not live near enough to give the certificate back in person, there is an alternative procedure to follow.

First, send your broker the unsigned certificate (using certified return receipt mail). Your broker will then send you a "stock power," which is just like the back of your certificate. You then sign the stock power and mail it back to the broker. The broker staples this to the back of the original certificate, which is now ready to be traded.

Obviously, this process takes a long time. This is why most certificates are kept in street name so that they can be traded, with your permission, at any moment.

HOW LONG DO I HAVE BETWEEN THE TIME I PLACE AN ORDER AND WHEN I ACTUALLY PAY FOR IT?

You have five business days. Suppose you order 100 shares of XYZ Company at $85 a share on Monday, November 9th. You will have to pay for them by Monday, November 16th, the fifth business day following the trade date (the date of your original transaction). November 16th is the settlement date, meaning not only does the trade have to be fully paid for, but the securities must be delivered to the brokerage firm from wherever the stock was purchased.

When securities are sold, the cash will be credited into your account on the settlement date, at which time your broker will send you a check.

SUPPOSE I BOUGHT 100 SHARES OF XYZ FOR $85 ON MONDAY, NOVEMBER 9TH, AND ON TUESDAY THE 10TH I WANT TO SELL THEM FOR $90. CAN I DO THAT?

Yes you can, but you can't receive your profit until you have fully paid for the stocks you ordered. You must still send your broker $8,500 for the 100 XYZ shares within five business days. When the trade is paid for, the broker can then send you $9,000 after the sell trade settles November 17th, five business days after November 10th. Not adhering to this procedure is known as "freeriding," and is not allowable under any circumstances.

CAN I SELL A STOCK TO ESTABLISH A LOSS FOR TAX PURPOSES AND THEN BUY IT RIGHT BACK?

If you sell a stock and establish a loss, you must wait at least 31 days before buying the same security or a similar security, or the IRS will disallow the loss. Also, you must not have purchased the same or similar security within

31 days prior to the sale in order to make use of the loss. This is known as the Wash Sale Rule.

HOW DO I CHECK ON THE VALUE OF SOME OLD STOCK CERTIFICATES I FOUND?

Many people think that because a stock is not listed in the financial section of the newspaper, it is worthless. Companies are frequently bought and sold, merged with other companies, disappear and reappear with new names and logos. Old certificates may still have value under a different company name.

Tracking that down is not as difficult as it appears. The first approach involves going to a public library to see the *Directory of Obsolete Securities* and the *Financial Stock Guide Service*. Both are published by Financial Information Inc. of Jersey City, New Jersey. These volumes list obsolete stocks and their successor companies. You should be able to find out if your stock is still active and which transfer agent (a bank or trust company responsible for record keeping and the registration and reregistration of available stock certificates) deals with it.

Many local brokerage houses will check a stock for you free of charge unless extensive research is necessary. There are professional firms which will charge fees of approximately $50 to check out a company. This might be worth the expense, particularly if your stock was issued before 1927. In any event, don't consider it wallpaper until you are sure it has no value.

HOW DO I KEEP TRACK OF ALL MY DEALINGS WITH MY BROKER?

Every month you will receive a statement of your account (or every three months if you are not transacting any business). The statement will list your name and mailing address, Social Security number, account number, brokerage firm name, and broker's name. It will also show your current positions, if any, and any cash balance or debits. Positions refer to the stocks, bonds, mutual funds, etc., which you have bought or sold. If you have a margin account (see page 82), any debits or money lent to you will be shown, along with any interest charges. Any activity in your account, such as deposits or withdrawals, interest, or dividends, will be shown on your account statement.

WHAT IF THERE'S AN ERROR ON MY STATEMENT?

The first thing to do is to double-check your statement against your own records. You should keep all prior statements, and all trade confirmations you receive from your broker. If your records do not match up with your current statement, call your broker. Be sure you have your records in front of you when you call in case you need to refer to them.

Ask your broker if she can explain the error to you. Both you and your broker have equal responsibility in seeing that your statement is maintained accurately.

WHAT IS THE W-9 FORM I RECEIVE FROM MY BROKER?

A W-9 tax form is sent to you for your signature and must be returned to your broker. If this is not done, the firm is required to withhold 20 percent of any future proceeds in your account for tax purposes.

I'M INTERESTED IN BUYING OR SELLING A PARTICULAR STOCK. HOW DO I GET A QUOTE FROM MY BROKER?

Suppose you are interested in buying stock in General Motors and you call your broker for a price quote. One broker may say, "General Motors is now at 30 by 30⅛." Another broker might answer, "General Motors is bid at 30 and offered at 30⅛." Both brokers are saying the same thing, but what do they mean?

Both statements mean that General Motors is being sold at $30 per share, and is being bought at $30.125 per share. If you wanted to buy GM stock, you would pay 30⅛, which is also known as the offer or the ask. If you were selling your GM stock, you would receive the bid, or $30.00 per share.

HOW DO I LEARN TO READ THE FINANCIAL PAGES?

Although most of the material printed on newspaper financial pages is direct and rather simple, the headings are not always adequately explained. For example, in a typical table you will find a stock listed by its acronym (initials), not its full name, because of the limited space available. You might see the high and low price for the stock for the current year or for the last 12 months. Dividend rates are often included, as are the ratios or relationships between the earnings of the company and the price for which the share is sold, which is known as the Price to Earnings Ratio. The high, low and closing prices for the day, along with the change of price from the previous day, are usually also included (see following table). Stock listings (the symbols used to identify the stock) never change; however, abbreviated names for listed stocks can vary from one newspaper to the next depending on the space they have available.

52-Week				Yld	PE	Sales				
High	Low	Stock	Div	%	Ratio	100s	High	Low	Last	Ch
5¾	3¼	Dansha	...		9	70	4⅞	4⅝	4⅝	−⅜
15½	9⅝	Ejay	.48	4.3	16	14	11¼	11⅛	11¼	+⅛

For instance, you would read the above excerpt as follows (stocks listed above are for fictitious companies): During the past 52 weeks, the highest price for Dansha (Danshar Corp.) stock was 5¾ ($5.75), and the lowest was 3¼ ($3.25). There was no dividend or yield for this stock. The price-to-earnings ratio was 9. There were 7,000 shares sold (70 x 100) that day. The highest price the stock brought on that day was 4⅞ ($4.875), and the lowest price was 4⅝ ($4.625). The last price (or the last trade made) on that day was 4⅝. The price of this stock went down ⅜ from the last trade made on the previous day.

During the past 52 weeks, the highest price for Ejay (Ellen James and Co.) stock was 15½ ($15.50), and the lowest was 9⅝ ($9.625). The dividend was $.48, and the yield was 4.3 percent for this stock. The price-to-earnings Ratio was 16, and there were 1,400 shares sold (14 x 100) that day. The highest price that stock brought on that day was 11¼ ($11.25), and the lowest price was 11⅛ ($11.125). The last price (or the last trade made) on that day was 11¼. The price of this stock went up ⅛ from the previous day.

SHOULD I BE CHECKING THE STOCK PRICES IN THE NEWSPAPER EVERY DAY?

This depends on your investment personality, and your relationship with your broker. If slight fluctuations give you palpitations, you probably shouldn't look so often, because the market changes several times during the course of one day. You need to give your broker, and your investments, time to accomplish your goals. If you're unhappy with your broker's suggestions, however, tell him so, and if you continue to be unhappy, change brokers.

Being aware of your investment psychology can help you make appropriate investment decisions. If you're going to go into a panic every time the stock market fluctuates, stocks may not be a good investment for you. Picture yourself in the following situation: You bought 50 shares of IBM at $115 per share. The market goes up and IBM is now at $122 per share. Do you feel as though you should sell, take your profit, and go on to buy another stock? Suppose you decide to hold on. Now the market drops and IBM is $90 a share. Do you call your broker to ask his opinion of the future for this company, or decide you've lost enough money and sell? Your gut reaction to the normal fluctuations of the market is an important indication of your risk tolerance. If you're willing to take a long-term approach, stocks may be a good investment for you.

SHOULD I BE BUYING AND SELLING STOCKS FREQUENTLY?

Stock prices change every day. That doesn't mean you should be buying and selling every day. Your broker makes money every time you make a transaction. Be aware of how many times your broker wants to shift your investments—shifting may be more to his benefit than to yours. You might make more money holding on to your stock for the long term.

WHAT IS THE BEST APPROACH TO INVESTING IN STOCKS?

The best approach is one in which stocks are just one part of your investment portfolio, and are viewed as long-term investments. For example, if your investment approach is to accumulate blue chip stocks, then you might start with 100 shares of AT&T. You can then begin to add to your portfolio by reinvesting all distributions or dividends into the purchase of more shares. You may then decide that you will invest an additional $100 quarterly to further increase the number of shares you own. You can then choose another company and repeat the process. Depending upon how much money is available to you, you can accumulate 5 to 10 stocks with companies that have had good growth records in the past and are projected to continue their growth.

A basic investment portfolio should not be viewed as one that is constantly being traded. You should have a long term approach and, unless something dramatic occurs within a particular company, you should plan to hold its stock for at least 10 years.

WHAT IS THE DIFFERENCE BETWEEN A TRADER AND AN INVESTOR?

A stock trader is interested in the immediate profits generated by the buying and selling of stocks. That could mean the purchase of 1,000 shares of a stock at $10 per share one morning, and the sale of the same 1,000 shares at $11 per share the same day. A trader is looking for short-term profits.

Here is where your investment psychology plays an important part. Trading stocks can be very exciting, as well as very rewarding—but it is also very risky. If your broker is encouraging you to do a lot of trading, you must be sure that he has your interests at heart and not his own. Frequent buying and selling generates high commissions, which must be taken into account when assessing profits. A trader does not necessarily make riskier investments, he only trades more frequently.

An investor is more concerned with the long-term results of his investment. He looks at and is concerned with the overall performance of the company. He is, of course, also looking to make a profit, but is willing to wait longer to see a return.

WHAT IS INSIDER TRADING?

Insider trading is having knowledge or information that the public is unaware of and using this information to your advantage. For example, a company whose stock is worth $5 a share has just received a contract for new business that will greatly enhance the company's revenues, making the stock worth at least $10 a share. This has not yet been announced by the company, but your broker's sister is the secretary to the vice president of the company, and she tells your broker about the pending deal. He buys the stock at $5 per share. Next week the company announces the new contract and the stock jumps to $10. He then sells the stock and makes a handsome profit.

Insider trading is illegal and subject to fines, imprisonment, or both. Brokerage firms, brokers, institutions, corporations, etc., cannot use confidential information, not yet made public, to establish profits or beneficial losses because of insider trading regulations.

I'VE HEARD THE TERM "SELLING SHORT." WHAT DOES THAT MEAN?

Selling short means selling securities that you either 1) do not possess and therefore must borrow from your broker or 2) do possess, but do not wish to deliver. The former is the typical short-sale arrangement used if you think that a stock is about to drop in price. The latter is called "selling short against the box" and it is not used as frequently.

WHEN MIGHT YOU WANT TO SELL SHORT?

You might choose to sell short if you think that a stock is about to drop in price (for instance, if you know that a company is about to announce some bad news). Suppose you hear a rumor that ABC Inc.'s highly-touted new invention doesn't work after all. So you borrow 100 shares in ABC Inc. from your broker, and sell them at the market price of $100 per share. You now have $10,000. When the news gets out, ABC's stock drops to $50 per share. You buy 100 shares for $5,000, return them to your broker, and you have made $5,000.

WHEN WOULD YOU SELL SHORT AGAINST THE BOX?

This technique would be used to lock in a paper profit on a stock and postpone paying taxes on the capital gain. Here the investor borrows an equal amount of stock from a broker and sells the stock short. This locks in the gain. Then, when the investor is ready to take the gain, the stock owned can be used to close out the short position.

WHAT ARE THE RISKS OF SELLING SHORT?

The risk of selling short is the reverse of the situation you expected; the stock price goes up. In our example of ABC stock, what if the rumor you heard is false, or if the company works out the bugs and gets the product on the market after all? ABC's stock then goes up to $200 per share. In order to return the shares you borrowed, you have to pay that price and take a loss of $10,000!

Selling short is risky business. You have to pay a lot of brokerage costs for buying and selling, as well as assume the risk that the stock will go up. In addition, short sellers are responsible for making up any dividends, rights, etc., that are declared on stock they have borrowed. This is definitely not a technique for a beginning investor to try.

WHAT IS A MARGIN ACCOUNT?

In a margin account, the customer does not supply all the capital needed to complete his purchases. The brokerage house lends him the balance. The Federal Reserve Board sets the maximum amount a brokerage house can lend a client. This is known as Regulation T, and is currently 50 percent.

Suppose you wished to purchase 100 shares of IBM at $85 a share, for a total of $8,500. You may borrow, or margin, up to 50 percent of that amount, or $4,250, from the brokerage house. Then you would deposit $4,250 of your own money into a margin account. You are charged interest on the amount borrowed, known as the debit balance. The brokerage house holds your securities as collateral.

A margin account also permits you to borrow against the stocks and bonds you hold at an interest rate one to three percent above the bank loan rate charged to brokers. Dividends and interest on the securities continue to be credited to your account.

WHAT IS THE DANGER IN A MARGIN ACCOUNT?

The greatest risk is in falling values in the account. For example, if the value of your stock were to drop, your broker would make a "margin call" and ask for additional cash or securities for deposit in your account. If you could not provide these, the broker has the right to sell securities in your account to re-establish the correct minimum.

WHAT IS A STOCK SPLIT?

Many times when a stock rises a great deal in dollar value per share, the issuing corporation will issue a "split." This merely increases your holdings, usually by two for one or three for one, and the price is adjusted accordingly. For example, a stock selling at $90 per share could split two for one with the new share price at $45, or three for one with the new share price at $30. The chief advantage is that the lowering of the price per share can stimulate sales of the stock to more investors.

WHAT IS A REVERSE SPLIT?

A reverse split is usually a sign that the company is not doing well. In a reverse split, you get fewer shares, but they're worth more. If your stock was selling at $1 per share, a five to one reverse split would give you one share at $5 instead of five shares at $1. Many companies that have reverse splits suffer from poor earnings and balance sheets. They hope the higher price per share will make the company look healthier.

WHAT IS INVESTMENT BANKING?

Investment banking is the process by which companies can raise money through the issuance of securities. For example, XYZ Company needs $5 million to expand their manufacturing plant, reduce some existing debt, and increase their advertising budget. They don't want to borrow the money and increase their interest payments, so they decide to offer shares of their company in the form of stocks in exchange for the $5 million they need. They enlist the services of an investment banker or investment banking firm (usually a brokerage firm) that will determine the price of the stock, the amount of stock to be offered, and how best the company should use the proceeds ($5 million).

The investment banker usually purchases all of the stock from the company at a discount, and then sells it to its clients and/or other brokerage firms that in turn sells the stock to their clients.

HOW DOES INVESTMENT BANKING AFFECT ME?

Investment banking firms naturally try to find promising fledgling companies. Investment banking provides a unique opportunity for investors to get involved in the ground floor of these fledgling companies. It also often allows investors to get in on large, well-known, and often very successful, privately held companies that are going public, such as recently happened with Marvel Comics and RJR Nabisco.

If you're interested in a stock being issued through an investment banking firm, be sure to ask questions about the company whose stocks are being offered, as well as the investment firm. Ask your broker what other issues the investment firm has backed, and how these companies and stocks have performed.

WHAT IS AN IPO?

An IPO is an Initial Public Offering, and represents the first time a company has publicly offered securities. The investment banker files an S-1 Registration Statement with the SEC in order for these securities to be offered. The SEC doesn't judge the company, or pass merit, but merely makes sure that there has been full and fair disclosure of all the company's records and earnings, the background of the company, its board of directors, and whether or nor there are any lawsuits pending against the company.

IPOs must be registered in each and every state in which they are to be sold. If a broker has a client in California who wishes to purchase this stock, then the issue (as well as the broker and the brokerage firm) must be registered in California. Registering the issue in various states is known as "Blue Skying" the issue. This takes place while waiting for the S-1 to become effective.

WHAT IS A RED HERRING?

A red herring is a preliminary prospectus that contains information similar to that contained in the S-1 statement. It is called a red herring because it is stated on the front cover, in bright red ink, that this is a preliminary prospectus only and it is subject to revision and completion. The investment banking firm sends the red herring to prospective clients who might be interested in learning about the company while waiting for the SEC's approval. Before the issue is approved, no solicitations to buy can be made by the investment banker.

WHAT IS AN INDICATION OF INTEREST?

If you choose to invest in this company, you can give your broker an "indication of interest" for the amount of stock you will buy *if and when* the issue becomes effective (another way of saying it has been approved). If and when the issue does become effective, the broker will let you know and put in your order. You may receive all or part of your order, depending on the demand.

For example, suppose there were one million shares issued. Brokers may have received indications of interest for two million shares. In that case, each investor would get half of what they initially requested. An indication of interest is not binding, and the broker must let you know before he places your order.

WHAT ARE THE RISKS OF INVESTING IN AN IPO?

Because the stock has not previously been offered to the public, there may be a weak demand for the stock, a very strong demand for the stock, or something in between. The price of the stock may go up or down dramatically depending on demand. Before you invest in an IPO, you should look carefully at the company's profile in the red herring/prospectus, look at the track record of the investment banker, and look at the initial price of the stock before deciding to invest. Some IPOs do extremely well, some do not.

IT'S THE END OF THE YEAR. HOW WELL HAVE I DONE?

Your last account statement will usually show the total interest received and dividends paid to you during the course of the year. This is ordinary income, and is taxable (unless it comes from a tax-free bond).

Your brokerage firm will also send you a proceeds statement, showing the total amount of all sales in your account. This is not your profit, it is the total dollar amount of all sales. To determine your profits, you must subtract the total cost of your purchases from that amount.

Suppose you bought five different stocks that cost you a total of $15,000, and during the course of the year you sold all five stocks for $25,000. You have a capital gain of $10,000. Stocks that you currently own and have experienced a loss or gain in value do not count for tax purposes. These are only "on paper" and you do not realize a capital gain or loss until you actually sell the stock.

SMART QUESTIONS TO ASK ABOUT BONDS

WHAT IS A BOND?

Basically, a bond is a "promise to pay" in which the issuing agency, be it government, municipal, or corporate, promises a given rate of interest for a specific length of time, and promises to repay the loan at maturity date. The holder of this debt instrument is called a creditor.

Take a U.S. Treasury Bond, for example. You can purchase a Treasury bond for as little as $1,000. Suppose, however, that you purchased a $10,000 bond with a ten-year maturity date. You are, in essence, lending the government that money for ten years. If the interest rate on the bond is 7.46 percent, you would receive $372.50 twice a year, and, in ten years, the government would repay you the $10,000. The income is taxable on your federal return, but not on your state and local returns.

HOW DOES A BOND DIFFER FROM A STOCK?

Bonds and stocks are very different. A stockholder owns a share in a company. A bondholder holds a "promise to pay" instrument. The borrower is required only to pay the annual interest and to pay the face amount of the bond on the maturity date. The bondholder receives no benefit if the company that borrows the money has a great year. In a case where the borrower defaults, the bondholder is a creditor of the corporation and must be paid before any stockholders are paid.

IS A BOND A GOOD INVESTMENT FOR ME?

While some people trade bonds for profit, most people use bonds to supplement their income. When you invest in bonds, you should be reasonably sure you can afford to hold onto them until maturity, or you might risk a substantial penalty.

The risk with bonds is not getting paid back if the outfit you "lent to" goes bankrupt. Many bonds today carry insurance in case that happens, so that bonds are a relatively safe investment, if held to maturity.

HOW ARE BONDS RELATED TO INTEREST RATES?

When interest rates fall, the value of an existing bond increases. Suppose you buy a $10,000 bond that is returning 8 percent interest. If the interest rate falls to 5 percent, your bond will be of greater value than newly issued bonds.

Conversely, when interest rates rise, the value of existing bonds decreases. So if you buy a $10,000 bond when the interest rate is 5 percent, and then rates go up to 8 percent, your bond will decrease in value.

WHAT IS A BEARER BOND?

A dollar bill in your pocket is a bearer instrument. It is not registered to a specific person; whoever holds it is the owner. Similarly, a Bearer Bond is a bond issued without any registered owner named. It is usually a municipal obligation containing coupons which must be clipped and taken to the bank for redemption. New bonds issued by municipalities are no longer being issued in bearer form since they are riskier, because there is no registered owner and if lost or stolen, are negotiable.

In an attempt to reduce the risk of loss in selling stolen bearer bonds, many brokerage houses now require proof of ownership, such as the original purchase slip, in order to sell bearer bonds. This extra step, not necessary with a registered bond, is one of the many reasons bearer bonds are now so rare.

WHAT IS A BOOK ENTRY BOND?

Book Entry refers to the more common way in which bonds are issued today. The entry for the purchases made in the brokerage account are similar to the way an entry is made in a bankbook. The holder has a statement which says he owns the bond but there is no actual physical bond issued.

Book entry bonds were created to reduce the mountains of paperwork that surround bond purchases. It simplifies buying and selling bonds because no certificate has to change hands. It is an electronic exchange between buyer and seller, similar to when a bank wires funds to another bank.

HOW DO I BUY OR SELL A BOND?

All bonds are bought and sold through stockbrokers. You would call your broker, place the order, and pay for the trade on the settlement date, which is usually five business days after the date of purchase. Buying a bond (or selling one) is a very simple process. Many banks now have brokerage departments which allow you to buy or sell bonds through their offices.

HOW ARE BONDS RATED?

Since it would be almost impossible for you as an individual to judge the financial soundness of a city or corporation selling bonds, there are bond-rating services that do that job for you. The three largest are Moody's, Standard & Poor's, and Duff & Phelps. Ratings run from

Aaa to C at Moody's, from AAA to D at Standard and Poor's, and from Aaa to Ccc minus at Duff & Phelps. Triple A ratings are the best, and a first-time bond buyer would do well to stick with double or triple A bonds. Bonds with lower ratings usually offer higher yields, but greater risk.

CAN A BOND'S RATINGS CHANGE?

Yes. As each of the rating services does their review of the company's or the municipality's ability to pay on its bond obligations, it rates their financial soundness. As the ability to pay improves, the rating changes positively to reflect this change. However, when questions arise— either as a result of business difficulties for a company or budget deficit for a municipality—the rating can fall. The more severe the problem, the lower the rating. The lower the rating, the greater the risk to the investor. If you already own a bond and its rating is lowered, the value of your bond decreases.

WHAT ARE TAX-FREE BONDS?

Tax-free bonds are bonds that pay interest which is exempt from taxation. This exemption could be from federal, state, or local taxes, or all three at the same time. If you're buying bonds, be sure to ask your broker to explain all the tax ramifications to you.

Most municipal bonds (bonds issued by cities, states, counties or municipalities) are exempt from federal income taxes. Some municipal bonds are subject to alternative minimum tax (AMT). Check with your tax advisor. In most cases, they're also exempt from state and local income taxes in the state in which they were issued. Thus, bonds issued by Indiana, for example, would be exempt from Indiana income tax but not from Massachusetts income tax. Bonds issued by the U.S. government are not exempt from Federal income tax, but they are exempt from state and local income tax.

ARE MUNICIPAL BONDS INSURED?

Some bonds are insured; most bonds, however, are not. Those that are insured will pay a smaller yield than those that are not. The difference in yield is used to pay the "insurance premium." The most common municipal bond insurers are the Municipal Bond Insurance Association (MBIA) and the Municipal Bond Acceptance Corporation (AMBAC). Private insurance companies occasionally insure bonds as well. If you're interested in investing in municipal bonds, be sure to ask your broker if they are insured. (For more information on municipal bonds, see Section 4.)

SHOULD I BUY UNINSURED BONDS? HOW RISKY ARE THEY?

As stated earlier, all bonds are rated. Ratings range from AAA at the top, down to NR, or nonrated, which is the lowest. Any bond rated A or better is considered "institutional quality," which means that they are judged to be able to meet their required interest payments and repayment at maturity. All bond ratings are subject to change, therefore insured bonds provide greater stability and security—at a higher price. However, any bond of institutional quality is considered a very low risk.

WHAT IS A CORPORATE BOND?

When a corporation borrows from the public, it's called a bond issue. You buy the bond for a certain amount, say $5,000, and when it matures you get back $5,000. But in the meantime, you get the stated interest rate twice a year.

WHAT KINDS OF CORPORATE BONDS ARE THERE?

There are basically two categories of corporate bonds. The first is a straight bond (or debenture). Similar to most government and municipal bonds, these pay interest semiannually to maturity, whereupon your capital is returned to you. The second is a convertible bond, which can be exchanged, at any time, for a fixed number of shares of the issuing company's common stock. The appreciation or depreciation of the company's common stock will influence the price of the convertible bond as well.

DO YOU GET A BETTER RETURN ON THE CORPORATE BONDS?

The corporate bond is different from the municipal bond. To begin with, the corporate bond has no tax advantage—all the interest you receive is taxable. Also, corporate bonds are paid with corporate revenues, while municipal bonds are paid by the taxing power of the municipality. Therefore, corporate bonds are perceived as possessing a greater risk, and so paying a greater return. This isn't always the case, since the interest rate remains constant, and at maturity the capital should be returned to you.

WHAT DOES IT MEAN WHEN A BOND IS CALLABLE?

A callable bond allows the issuing corporation or municipality to call back, or ask that their bonds be returned to them, prior to the date of maturity. This means that the issuing agency can demand that you return your bonds to them. They will pay you the face value of the bond, but you lose any interest you would have earned had you been allowed to keep the bond for several more years.

Suppose you have a $10,000 bond with a maturity date of 2005, and a callable date of 1994. At the callable date, the issuing agency has the right to ask you to return all, or a portion, of your bond.

WHY WOULD A CORPORATION OR A MUNICIPALITY CALL A BOND?

An issuing agency might call your bonds because interest rates have dropped. If the agency can buy back your bonds, which are paying you 8 percent interest, and sell new ones for 5 percent, they will certainly do so. If this sounds a little bit like refinancing a house, it is.

Another reason your bonds might be called is that the project for which these bonds were issued has paid a large profit. The issuer will then want to pay off the bonds early so it doesn't have to keep paying out interest.

Many bonds are callable. Some even have several call

dates (dates on which the agency can exercise its right to call the bonds), so be sure to ask your broker if the bonds you're considering are callable.

WHAT IS A BOND TRUST?

A bond trust contains many different bonds with varying interest rates and maturity dates. This widens the "risk" and returns capital in a "serial" way as each bond in the trust matures.

For example, a municipal bond trust may contain as many as 40 different bonds with various interest rates and maturity dates—some at 5 percent, some at 6 percent, some at 7 percent, some maturing in 1995, some maturing into the year 2000 and some maturing as far as 2030. There may be some callable bonds, but a trust allows for a blending of the various rates and time periods of maturity so that you get your investment back over a period of time, rather than in one lump sum. Most brokerage houses offer municipal funds and trusts. Some investment companies, such as John Nuveen & Co., specialize in this area.

WHAT ARE SHORT- AND LONG-TERM TRUSTS?

A short-term trust is one that will show you a relatively quick return. For example, you can purchase a municipal bond trust that will mature in as little as 15 years. You might begin to get income on a monthly, quarterly, or semiannual basis right away, and see the maturity of the first bonds within the first three or four years.

A long-term trust, on the other hand, usually doesn't begin to return your principal for 10 or 15 years.

I NEED INCOME. WHICH TYPE OF TRUST IS BEST FOR ME?

The easy answer is that the trust paying the highest income is the best, and usually that means a long-term trust. There are other circumstances that influence your decision about which trust to buy, however. The short-term trust returns principal earlier, and as a result fluctuates less in price. This could be important if the possibility exists that you might have to sell these assets before all the principal is returned. Since short-term trusts generally pay less income, the decision really hinges on your need for "immediate" income versus the need for principal before the maturity of the bonds in the trust.

WHAT IS A BOND FUND?

A bond fund combines many different bonds (also called issues), but it differs from the trust in that it is actively managed and continuously buys and sells bonds. The manager is generally an investment company, usually referred to as a mutual fund company (for more information on mutual funds, see page 104). That company selects one person or a group of people to oversee the investment of clients' money.

A bond fund has no stated maturity date. You purchase shares in the fund, and you may buy or sell at any time. The price per share fluctuates with the interest rate; therefore, there is absolutely no guarantee that the price per share at which you purchased the fund will be the price per share when you wish to sell. So if you purchase when interest rates are high, and then wish to sell when interest rates are low, you may lose money.

HOW CAN I CHECK ON THE PERFORMANCE OF A PARTICULAR BOND FUND?

The same sources you would use to evaluate stock funds are also the sources for bond fund performance results. Funds managers are judged by the net total return of their portfolio management: Bottom line—has the fund made money? Many fund companies reward their managers with bonus dollars for good management since good performance figures encourage additional investors.

ARE BUYING SHARES IN BOND FUNDS RISKIER THAN BUYING STOCK FUNDS?

The risks in buying bonds are related to changes in interest rates and bond quality. When interest rates increase, bond fund share prices go down. When interest rates decrease, bond fund share prices go up. If the choice of a good bond fund such as a government bond fund is made, quality will never be a problem. However, with many bond funds, you must depend on good managers to prevent capital losses. The other risk in bond funds is that of matching inflation and buying power. All bonds are investments which historically do not match the buying power of stocks. Stock funds can be riskier in that there is more volatility in the stock market than in the bond market.

WHAT ARE CLOSED-END BOND FUNDS?

A closed-end fund (both stock and bond funds)

resembles a corporation more than a typical mutual fund in that it issues a fixed number of shares that can only be acquired or sold on the stock market. (Shares in a traditional, or open-end mutual fund, can be purchased directly from the fund itself.) You trade shares in the closed-end fund the way you do with stock, paying a commission to the broker when you buy or sell.

WHAT DOES IT MEAN WHEN A BOND IS PURCHASED AT A DISCOUNT?

Discounted bonds are bonds that are purchased at a price under their face value, or "below par." The opportunity to purchase such bonds occurs when current interest rates are higher than the interest rate on the bond that is for sale. For example, suppose you have a $10,000 bond returning 5 percent interest. You would get $500 a year in interest from that bond. However, if new bonds of the same quality were sold at 8 percent, their buyers would get $800 per year.

If you wanted to sell your 5 percent bond, no one would buy it at full price, because they could get a higher interest rate by purchasing a newer bond. In order to sell your bond, you would have to sell it at less than face value. You would sell it for $9,150. The purchaser would still get $500 per year (for a current yield of 5.4%), and at maturity in 2005 would collect the full $10,000.

Discounted bonds are best suited for investors seeking a moderate level of current income, but not the maximum available. In exchange for lower income, these investors receive capital appreciation when the bond grows from its discounted price to the higher face amount at maturity.

WHAT ARE THE REASONS FOR SELLING BONDS AT A DISCOUNT?

If you need money immediately and cannot wait until the bond's maturity date, you may have to sell your bond at a discount. You then must sell regardless of price. If interest rates in the marketplace are higher than the interest rate promised on your bond, you will have to sell it at a discount.

WHEN AND HOW IS THIS AN ADVANTAGE OR A DISADVANTAGE?

Selling a bond at a discount is obviously a disadvantage when you lose the full value of the bond because you have to sell it prematurely. Selling a bond at a discount can be an advantage when used as a tax swap, as discussed later on in this section.

THEN WHAT IS A PREMIUM BOND?

A premium bond is the exact opposite of a discount bond. In the previous example, your bond was paying less interest than new bonds being offered. With a premium bond, your rate of interest would be higher than the interest new bonds were offering. Suppose the bond you bought paid 8 percent interest to June 15, 2005, and then the rates dropped to 5 percent. Someone could buy your bond and make more interest than if he bought a newly issued bond. But to make it worth your while to sell, he would have to pay you more than the face value of your bond.

This additional cost to buy the bond is called the premium. So if your bond was paying 8 percent per year (or $800), and new bonds were paying 5 percent, an investor would have to pay you $11,700 for that same bond—an $1,700 premium over the face amount of $10,000. At maturity, the investor receives $10,000. However, he has received $3,900 more interest over the life of the bond.

WHAT IS A BOND SWAP?

When interest rates are dramatically higher or lower it is sometimes recommended as a tax strategy that a "swap" or exchange be made of an existing bond for another. For example, if you held a $10,000 bond that was selling at a severe discount, you could sell the bond for $6,500, incur a capital loss for tax purposes, and immediately buy another bond of like quality with either a different interest rate or maturity date but with the same initial face amount. For $6,500 you could buy someone else's $10,000 discounted bond. Of course, you will experience capital gains at the bond's maturity and taxes will be due then. But postponement of taxation has always been the game—and this one works.

WHAT EXACTLY IS A CAPITAL LOSS OR CAPITAL GAIN?

Capital loss and gain occurs when you sell your investment. In the example above, you bought a bond for $10,000 and sold it for $6,500. In that case, the price at which you sold your investment is less than the price you paid for it; therefore, you now have a capital loss of $3,500. If, however, you had sold your bond for more than you paid for it, you would have a capital gain. So if you sold your $10,000 bond for $13,500 you would have a capital gain of $3,500. No gain or loss occurs for tax purposes unless an actual sale has taken place. Any profit or loss on paper is considered an "unrealized" occurrence.

WHAT KINDS OF BONDS CAN BE SWAPPED?

Corporate bonds can be swapped for other corporate bonds; municipal bonds for other municipal bonds. This is generally done when taking a tax loss is most advantageous to you. The future capital gain that comes when the new bond matures will hopefully find you in a lower tax bracket than you are in now (for instance, when you are retired).

WHO DOES THE BOND SWAP?

When a bond is sold as a tax consideration, the broker will sell the bond in the open market to another bond trader. The broker will generally earn a commission for executing the transaction. When the broker buys a new bond to replace the old bond, another commission is generated. This commission can be from ½ percent to 3 percent of the face amount of the bond. A bond swap is a fairly sophisticated process, but when done properly it is a very effective tax and portfolio strategy.

WHAT ARE ZERO-COUPON BONDS?

A zero-coupon bond is by definition the same as any other bond. It has a face amount, an interest rate, and a maturity date; however, it is issued at a deep discount from its maturity value and pays no interest during the life of the bond. The stated interest, or "coupon" on the bond is 0 percent. This is the most severe example of a discounted bond. Since it pays no current interest, all the benefits come from the increase in value from its purchase price and the maturity value.

Zero-coupon bonds are issued by the U.S. government, corporations, and municipalities. Zero-coupon bonds are the most sensitive to changes in interest rates, both positively and negatively. When interest rates increase, the value of these bonds falls the most, especially when there is a long time until maturity. However, when interest rates fall, these bonds will grow faster than any others. Zero-coupon bonds are best for investors seeking capital appreciation with no concern for current income. They are frequently used for asset accumulation for retirement accounts or college education expenses. Speculators seeking to take advantage of declining interest rates will also buy zero-coupon bonds.

WHO SHOULD BUY ZERO-COUPON BONDS?

Zero-coupon bonds are most appropriate as the foundation in an educational funding plan and retirement or pension plans. Since they are fixed investments and will not match future investments for buying power, they should be a part of a larger investment portfolio. Zero-coupon bonds usually fluctuate a great deal with changes in interest and can be utilized by the more sophisticated investor as a trading vehicle to produce capital gain. This is not a strategy for the beginning investor.

WHAT ARE U.S. SAVINGS BONDS?

Savings bonds are issued by the U.S. Government in two types: Series EE, which accumulate in value similar to zero-coupon bonds, and Series HH, which pay a monthly income over the life of the bond. Savings bonds have an advantage no other type of bond has—they offer a choice of current taxation or tax deferral. At the time of purchase, you can choose to have your interest taxed annually, or to defer taxation until the bonds are redeemed. Other bonds, including zero-coupon bonds, require that you pay tax annually on interest paid or accrued. Municipal bond interest is not taxable; however, tax could be due if the bond is sold prior to maturity.

Recent legislation has provided tax relief for savings bond investors using the money for college education expenses. The rules are strict in establishing who qualifies, so ask for help from a tax advisor to determine if you qualify.

WHICH BONDS ARE CONSIDERED MOST SAFE? WHICH ARE CONSIDERED LEAST SAFE?

The safest bonds are obligations of the United States Treasury and insured municipal bonds. The next safest are the AAA governmental agency obligations and corporate bonds. The least safe are those classified as "junk."

WHAT ARE JUNK BONDS?

Junk bonds are issues that sell at relatively low prices because of the low credit ratings of their issuers. Due to their low ratings and high risk, these bonds offer interest rates well above normal. For example, many bonds issued during the takeover frenzy of the '80s were yielding 15 to 17 percent interest. Of course, the risk is in their ability to continue interest payments and their ability to redeem the bonds at maturity.

SMART QUESTIONS TO ASK ABOUT MUTUAL FUNDS

WHY SHOULD I INVEST IN MUTUAL FUNDS?

Mutual funds provide a way for the small investor to have a professionally managed, diversified portfolio. There are many different kinds of mutual funds with many different investment objectives. For example, if you are looking for a comparatively safe, steady income stream, you might invest in a bond fund (or any kind of mutual fund that concentrates its investments into securities which provide interest or dividend payments).

If you are more interested in seeing your capital grow, you would look for a growth fund that concentrates its investments in securities that are likely to appreciate.

If you need some immediate income but also want capital growth in your investment, you would invest in a balanced, or growth and income, fund where you could take your dividends and reinvest all your gains.

WHAT IS THE PRINCIPAL ADVANTAGE OF INVESTING IN MUTUAL FUNDS?

For small investors, mutual funds make a lot of

sense—not because the mutual fund will invest any more wisely than you would on your own, but because the fund's holdings are more diversified than yours would probably be. If you've got limited funds, and you don't want to pay a fortune in commissions buying and selling, you'll probably only invest in one or two securities—and that can be risky. If something goes wrong, all your eggs are in one basket. Mutual funds give you instant diversification by putting your "eggs" in many different baskets. If something goes wrong with one investment you have opportunities to make up your losses in one of the others. That is really how a mutual fund protects the small investor.

WHY IS DIVERSIFICATION IMPORTANT?

Most people do not have adequate funds to invest in a large variety of companies. Mutual funds allow you, as a small investor, to participate in a large pool of companies to a much greater degree than you could probably ever do on your own. Most importantly it makes investment cost effective: fees are held to a minimum because you can invest in many different securities without having to pay a fee for each individual investment.

ARE THERE OTHER ADVANTAGES TO INVESTING IN MUTUAL FUNDS?

Mutual Funds also provide you with experienced portfolio managers who have track records of past performance that you can review (see next question). Most professional money managers will not accept individual investments of under $100,000. By investing in a mutual fund, you can utilize the services of a professional money manager with as little as $500 (and sometimes less) to invest.

WHAT ARE THE DISADVANTAGES OF INVESTING IN MUTUAL FUNDS?

Probably the greatest disadvantage is that you have no active participation in selection of any stocks. (Some people view passive involvement as a positive and not a negative, because it relieves them of having to make decisions in areas in which they feel insecure or ill informed.)

And, although mutual funds are professionally managed, the performance of the fund (how well it does overall) is based on the judgment and experience of the one person (or in some cases the team of individuals) who manages the fund—and the current manager may not always be the one who created the past successful performance. If the fund in which you want to invest has changed managers recently or frequently, ask your broker why this has happened.

WHAT IS THE GREATEST DANGER IN INVESTING IN MUTUAL FUNDS?

As with any investment in equities, your biggest danger is the loss in value of your shares themselves. Your net asset value can never be guaranteed.

WHAT IS THE PROCEDURE FOR INVESTING IN A MUTUAL FUND?

Before you invest in a mutual fund, you should request, receive, and read carefully, a prospectus which fully describes the composition of the fund, its goals and objectives, and all charges relating to the purchase of shares in the fund. Shares can then be purchased directly from the fund, or through a stockbroker.

When your account is opened, your shares are issued at that day's closing prices. The next day, the portfolio managers put your money to work. Your funds may or may not pay interest or dividends regularly as well as capital gains. If you do receive interest or dividends, you may keep them as income, or you may reinvest them in additional shares.

If you wish to sell your shares, you may do so by telephone or by mail. The price you receive is the closing Net Asset Value per share at the close of business on the day your order is received.

HOW CAN I RESEARCH PAST PERFORMANCE OF MUTUAL FUNDS?

SEC rules provide that every fund must make a prospectus available to investors. Before you make any fund investment, you should review this material. Your stockbroker or financial planner will usually have this information for you.

Information is also readily available at your public library. Among the most frequently used resources is the *Standard & Poor's/Lipper Mutual Fund Guide*. This publication issues quarterly reports and considers things like volatility and total return, etc. *Morning Star*, a trade publication, issues a mutual fund source book which measures risk and is designed to indicate the potential performance, both positive and negative, of various funds. The

Wiesenberger Report issues a mutual fund investment analyzer on a monthly basis which provides graphic illustrations of how a fund performs relative to its peers and to the market in general. *The No-Load Investor* is a monthly newsletter which covers the performance of 644 no-load and low-load mutual funds.

Periodicals such as *Money Magazine*, *Forbes*, *Changing Times*, *Barron's*, etc., issue quarterly reports on the top performers in both stock and bond mutual funds.

WHAT'S THE BEST WAY TO READ A PROSPECTUS? IT LOOKS SO CONFUSING!

The most important part of a prospectus is the information about the fund manager, or management team, in relation to past performance. Look carefully at the investment objectives of the portfolio manager and the strategies that are going to be employed. For example, if it is a bond fund, in what quality bonds will they invest? Will they use options (see Section 5) in an attempt to increase the income? There should be no surprises if you read the prospectus. Disclosure of what the portfolio managers can and cannot do is clearly stated.

Another section which should be reviewed carefully is the cost and charges related to the investment. Every prospectus is very clear about the purchase fees and charges involved in the management of that particular fund portfolio. Be sure you are comparing "apples with apples," however. You cannot compare a bond fund with an aggressive growth fund and expect the charges to be similar. Charges reflect the turnover, or the number of transactions, that take place in the portfolio. The more frequently the portfolio manager is buying and selling (as in an aggressive growth fund), the higher the fees. If you are considering investing in a particular type of fund, be sure to read the prospectus of another similar fund to see how the fees compare.

If you are uncomfortable or uncertain about anything you have read, or are having any problems reading the prospectus, do not be afraid to ask questions.

WHAT KINDS OF FEES ARE INVOLVED WITH MUTUAL FUNDS?

All fees involved in the operation of a mutual fund portfolio are listed in the prospectus, in the summary of fund expenses. Fees might include the sales charge and the annual fund operating expenses, which would include management fees and 12B-1 fees along with other operating expenses. (The 12B-1 fee is $1/4$ to $1/2$ of a percentage point charge which is passed along to the broker who services the account in an attempt to encourage brokers to service these accounts through many years.)

HOW DO I KEEP SALES CHARGES TO A MINIMUM?

The larger your investment, the lower your sales charges will be. Usually, your sales charge is lowered when you invest at least $25,000. That is known as a "breakpoint." Other breakpoints are at $50,000, $100,000, $250,000, etc. Be sure to look in the prospectus or to ask your advisor what the breakpoints are because it may be possible to lock in a lower sales charge with your initial investment if you intend to invest more later on, and will sign a letter of intent to that effect.

WHAT EXACTLY IS A LETTER OF INTENT, OR LOI?

The letter of intent is a method of assuring a reduced sales charge at the initial purchase by signing a statement saying you intend to make additional investments (usually within a 13-month period). For example, if the breakpoint level is $25,000 and your initial investment is $10,000, by signing a letter of intent your sales charges would be the same as if you had initially invested $25,000—but you must invest at least $15,000 more within 13 months.

If you should sell your fund shares before then, or fail to make the additional investment after 13 months, an additional sales charge would be assessed against your holdings.

HOW MUCH MONEY DO I NEED TO MAKE AN INVESTMENT IN A MUTUAL FUND?

There are some mutual funds that will take as little as $250 as a minimum investment. And many funds will allow you to make additional investments with as little as $25. This allows you to accumulate funds easily, which is particularly helpful if you're aiming at a specific goal, such as college funding or retirement.

WHAT KINDS OF PORTFOLIOS OR FUNDS ARE THERE?

The variety offered is quite large. Some funds invest in fixed income securities or instruments such as government obligations, corporate bonds or municipal bonds. Some invest in stocks issued by firms ranging from recognized blue chip growth companies like IBM, to small, unknown companies with more potential for growth.

There are now hundreds of different kinds of funds available, so that if you have a particular interest, you can usually find a corresponding fund in which to invest. If you are interested in environmental issues, for example, you can find several funds that invest in environmentally friendly organizations. Or if you are a collector of rare coins, you can probably find a "rare coin" fund. These kinds of funds are usually called specialty or sector funds.

WHAT IS A GROWTH FUND?

The primary objective of a growth fund is the increase in capital provided by managed investment in companies that are "growing." Current income (dividends) is not an issue here. Any income generated usually comes from capital gains.

WHAT IS AN INCOME FUND?

The primary goal of an income fund is to provide the investor with monthly income. The most popular of these are government securities and municipal bond funds, although there are corporate and global income funds as well. You may keep the interest income earned from such funds, or the income can be reinvested.

WHAT IS A BALANCED FUND?

A balanced fund is usually a combination growth and

income portfolio. That means that the fund purchases stocks in companies that are growing in value, and also purchases bonds that give off dividends regularly. Balanced portfolio managers are limited by the prospectus as to the percentage of investment that can be made in stocks and the percentage that must be used for purchasing bonds.

WHAT IS A GROWTH AND INCOME PORTFOLIO?

In a growth and income portfolio, growth is usually the primary objective with income secondary. Therefore the percentage of investment allowed for growth securities would be larger than that allowed for income-producing securities.

WHAT IS A TOTAL RETURN FUND?

In a total return fund the focus is on the ultimate investment performance, using both growth and income vehicles. It usually has more investment flexibility than either a balanced fund or a growth and income fund.

WHAT ARE HIGH YIELD FUNDS?

High yield funds usually involve more risk through the use of options (discussed in section 5) as an investment strategy, or through the use of lower-rated securities or bonds. These are frequently called "junk" portfolios. Because they involve more risk, they should also involve more research before any investment in such a fund is made.

WHAT ARE GLOBAL FUNDS?

Global funds, as the name suggests, involve investment instruments from around the world. You can buy global growth stock funds, global income funds, or global funds that balance stock and bond portfolios.

Along with the normal risks associated with these portfolios, there is the added risk/reward that comes from currency fluctuation. When the dollar is strong against foreign currencies, the value of shares increases more. Conversely, when the dollar is weak, the value of shares decreases regardless of the value in the underlying security.

WHAT IS AN ASSET ALLOCATION FUND?

With the growth in interest in foreign investing, funds which combine investment in both international and domestic stocks and bonds have recently been developed. The portfolio management allocates these investments in a way that allows them to take advantage of market conditions worldwide. For example, at any one time 20 percent of the investment funds might be in domestic stocks, 20 percent in domestic bonds, 30 percent in foreign stocks, 20 percent in foreign bonds and 10 percent in cash.

WHAT IS AN OPEN-END FUND?

An open-end fund issues an unlimited number of shares and will always repurchase them from you in the event you want to sell your shares.

WHAT IS A CLOSED-END FUND?

Closed-end funds issue only a limited amount of shares, and are usually sold on the stock exchange. You can purchase these shares only when and as available. When you want to redeem your shares, you have to wait for someone to be willing to buy before you can sell.

These funds appeal to some investors because the shares can sometimes can be purchased at a discount. For example, a portfolio's value, if all shares were completely sold, may be $25 per share (the liquidating value). You may find that shares are available for $20 each. This may appear to be a good buy; however, whereas open-end funds must repurchase shares from an investor who wishes to sell, there is no such redemption feature in a closed-end fund. Therefore, you may not find someone willing to pay you $20 (or even less) if and when you need to sell. Use extreme caution if you're thinking about investing in a closed-end fund.

WHAT ARE A MUTUAL MONEY MARKET FUND?

Money market funds are mutual funds that invest in large denomination short-term money market instruments issued by the Treasury Department, government agencies, banks, and various corporations. Mutual money market funds generally give higher returns than bank money markets, as well as instant liquidity. Most issue checkbooks to make it easy for you to withdraw your funds.

HOW SAFE IS A MUTUAL MONEY MARKET FUND?

The primary difference between mutual money market funds and any other money market fund is the degree of safety. Although most money market funds are not insured, those that invest in very short-term government obligations only, or U.S. Treasury and government agency obligations only, are usually considered very safe.

There are some mutual money market funds available that invest in a variety of accounts at banks, which are insured by the FDIC for the maximum $100,000 per account. Even if you had invested $100,000,000 in one money market fund, the fund would have spread out its investments over many accounts; therefore your entire investment would be insured.

On the other hand, aggressive, income-oriented mutual money market funds may invest in lower quality corporate bonds. Such funds can be risky; therefore greater care should be taken before investing.

All money market funds are sold by prospectus. Information relevant to investments used will be totally revealed. Be sure to read the prospectus *before* you invest, and if there's anything you don't understand, ask your broker to explain it to you.

WHAT IS A FRONT-END LOAD FUND?

A front-end load fund includes a sales charge at the time of purchase. Shares are offered at a price that includes a sales charge. The "NAV" or "Net Asset Value" of the share is the selling price of the share.

Suppose a fund is offering shares for $16.52. That is the price you pay for each share. When you sell your shares, however, the price you get, or the Net Asset

Value for each share, might be $15.61. The difference, or $.91, represents a 5.5 percent sales charge you paid when you bought the shares.

WHAT IS A BACK-END LOAD FUND?

A back-end load fund does not have an initial sales charge; however, there are deferred charges which will be assessed if the investment is terminated within a short period of time. For example, a fund will typically charge 3 percent of current market value if the investment is terminated after three years.

It is best to invest in a back-end load fund if you plan to hold your investment for more than five years, which allows you to avoid sales charges altogether. Otherwise, deferred charges can be high, since the 3 percent charge would be on the current and possibly increased value of your shares.

WHAT IS A NO-LOAD FUND?

Like discount brokerage houses, no-load funds do not utilize a middleman, and do not have sales charges attached. If you are an investor with a short-term objective, say five years or less, no-load funds can make a lot of sense. All of your invested dollars go to work for you. As with discount brokers, if you can make your own decisions and do not need the help or guidance of an advisor, some no-load funds might do just as well for you as funds which include a sales charge.

WHERE DO I PURCHASE NO-LOAD FUNDS?

Since no-load funds do not utilize brokers or agents to generate sales, they do a great deal of advertising. Most weekend papers contain large ads in the business section. The *Wall Street Journal* has ads daily. All funds have 800 phone numbers. *Money Magazine*, *Kiplinger's Changing Times*, *Forbes*, etc., periodically list all no-load funds along with their performance records and phone numbers. All investing is done directly through the fund.

HOW DO I COMPARE FUNDS TO SEE WHETHER A FRONT-END LOAD, A BACK-END LOAD, OR NO-LOAD MAKES MORE SENSE FOR MY PARTICULAR OBJECTIVES?

If you can make your own decisions, and if you do not plan to stay invested for more than five years, you may do very well in no-load funds. If long-term investment is your goal the back-end or front-end loads usually make more economic sense. However, no-load funds pay a lot for direct mail and other media advertising since that is the only way they can reach investors. Their operating expenses, therefore, can be higher and net results to you can turn out to be less than with a "loaded" fund. You should not make any investment based solely on its initial cost—be sure to examine and compare the net result of all your investment possibilities.

WHAT IS MEANT BY A FAMILY OF FUNDS?

When a group of various mutual funds comes under the auspices of one large investment company, it is called a family of funds. Some families of funds have less than ten different kinds of funds, or portfolios, available, while many have well over one hundred. These portfolios have a wide variety of objectives and goals. Each fund in the family is independent of one another, and each usually has its own portfolio manager.

WHAT ARE THE ADVANTAGES OF BUYING INTO A FAMILY OF FUNDS?

A fund is described as a "family" because it usually has many "members." For example, the Putnam group of funds contains over fifty independent mutual funds. Some have income as their objective, some growth, some foreign investment, etc. Most fund families permit exchange between different groups of stock and bond portfolios within their family.

Compare a mutual fund to a home with many rooms. You can come out of one room and into another very easily: so it is with mutual funds. If you so chose, you could remove money from a taxable-bond fund, move some to a tax-free fund and then move the rest to a blue-chip stock portfolio. For example, if you had $10,000 in a government securities fund, you could move $5,000 to a tax-free fund and $5,000 to the stock fund. There are many fund families that will permit exchanges without any fee, and some that charge a nominal fee of as little as $5.

I HAVE SEEN THE INITIALS ROA ON MUTUAL FUND APPLICATIONS. WHAT DOES THAT MEAN?

ROA (Rights Of Accumulation) means that you can reach a breakpoint (or lower sales charge), outside the usual 13-month period by virtue of the fact that fund families allow for the linking of different funds within their group. For example, suppose you have invested $10,000 in a mutual fund family's government fund in 1988, $5,000 in their stock fund in 1989, $5,000 in their balanced fund in 1990, and $5,000 in their treasury bill portfolio in 1991. All these investments would be "linked" together to reduce your sales charge on any new investments. This is similar to a bank that eliminates or reduces your checking fees if you also have money in a savings and/or money market account.

DO ANY MUTUAL FUNDS HAVE AUTOMATIC INVESTMENT PLANS?

There are many fund families that would be very happy to arrange an automatic withdrawal from your checking or savings account on a regular basis for investment purposes. You must, of course, give your bank authorization for the fund to make these withdrawals for you.

WHAT IF I WANTED TO REINVEST MY DIVIDENDS AND CAPITAL GAINS?

Most funds give you the option of reinvesting monies produced by your portfolio or any portion thereof. For example, suppose you have a fund that is currently providing you with $200 in monthly dividends. You can choose to receive $100 as income every month, and have the other $100 reinvested in the fund. As profits from sales in the portfolio are declared and paid out, they can also be reinvested in the fund. Most reinvestment is done at the Net Asset Value (NAV), which means, in effect, that you pay no sales charges even in a front load fund.

Suppose, for example, the purchase price of a share in a popular mutual fund on a particular day is $12.01. Suppose, on that same day, you decide to reinvest money you have earned from that fund. Your price per share might only be $11.35. In other words, you get an "insider's" price when you reinvest in the fund. Building shares by reinvestment is probably one of the easiest ways to accumulate capital.

IS IT POSSIBLE FOR ME TO RECEIVE A STEADY INCOME EVERY MONTH FROM A MUTUAL FUND?

Yes it is, in a process called systematic withdrawal, which allows you to remove as much as you want by selling the number of shares required to produce that cash flow. For example, suppose you have invested in a mutual fund that produces $100 in dividends—but you require $120 per month. Each month, the fund management will sell off however many shares it takes to provide you with that extra $20. This system can be very useful as a supplemental retirement source.

This approach, however, can use up your capital. Therefore, ideally you should never remove more than is being produced by the fund in order to maintain the capital base. When you use a balanced fund or growth and income fund it sometimes makes a lot of sense to take the income and reinvest capital gains in an attempt to constantly increase the capital base at work. By reinvesting the gains, you should have more invested dollars to produce income and gains. With more capital accumulated, you will be able to draw more income in the future while still maintaining your capital investment. This approach can be used as a way to deal with declining buying power and the need for added income later on.

I'VE BEEN TOLD THAT I SHOULD USE DOLLAR COST AVERAGING WHEN INVESTING. WHAT DOES THAT MEAN?

When you dollar cost average you invest an equal amount of money in a fund or group of funds at regular intervals. This approach can use the volatility of the market to your advantage, since your money buys more shares when prices are low and fewer shares when prices are high.

For example, suppose you have $500 periodically to invest. When a share price is $25, your $500 will buy you 20 shares. When a share price is $10, $500 will buy you 50 shares. The average price for your first 70 shares is $14.29 (your total investment divided by your total number of shares). Dollar cost averaging, particularly when done over a regulated period of time, really works.

HOW DO I USE DOLLAR COST AVERAGING WITHIN A MUTUAL FUND?

The most practical way to dollar cost average in a mutual fund is to open the account with a given amount of dollars and then make an absolute commitment to add a set amount of dollars every month to the fund. Many fund families will do the investing for you. For example, you can deposit $10,000 into a mutual fund money market and then ask the mutual fund to move $1,000 per month into their growth portfolio. The result is shares purchased over time at varying prices; therefore your average price per share is usually less than if you invested the entire $10,000 in one day.

WHAT IS VALUE AVERAGING?

Value averaging is a variation on dollar cost averaging. Instead of making a commitment to invest a set amount of dollars per month, you make a commitment to purchase a set number of shares in the fund per month. For example, you might say that you will purchase 100 shares every month, regardless of price. The theory is that although one month 100 shares may cost you $1,200 (or $12 per share), the next month 100 shares may cost you $918 (or $9.18 per share). Obviously, both dollar cost averaging and value averaging work best over long periods of time.

IS IT POSSIBLE FOR A MUTUAL FUND TO GO BROKE?

A mutual fund cannot go bankrupt or broke. Its assets can and will fluctuate in value, however, due to fluctuations in the value of the securities in which it invests.

WHAT ABOUT FRAUD? CAN I LOSE MY MONEY BECAUSE THE FUND MANAGER EMBEZZLES THE MONEY AND RUNS OFF TO THE BAHAMAS WITH HIS SECRETARY?

The Investment Company Act of 1940 provides many effective safeguards for investors in mutual funds. The Act subjects the fund management to many legal restrictions. Officers of the fund who have access to the securities of the fund company must obtain fidelity bonds, which means that the fund is insured against any losses due to employee dishonesty.

WHAT HAPPENS IF A BROKER OR BROKERAGE HOUSE WHICH IS HOLDING MY MUTUAL FUND SHARES GOES BANKRUPT?

Again, your mutual fund shares are safe. The assets in the fund belong to the shareholder and not to any brokerage firm. All registered broker/dealers are automatically members of the Securities Investor Protection Corporation (SIPC). The SIPC provides protection for as much as $500,000 for the accounts of each customer.

HOW DO I READ THE MUTUAL FUND SECTION IN THE NEWSPAPER?

Here is a sample excerpt from a Mutual Fund Quotations page in a newspaper (the fund names below are fictitious):

	NAV	Offer Price	NAV Chg
Amalgamate Mutual:			
BaGr p	12.97	13.62	+ .09
Denco p	10.02	10.52	+ .02
Clayton IRA-CIT:			
Falon f	2.59	NL	...
Chryst f	2.94	NL	- .02
Dunston:			
EnVel t	11.30	11.30	+ .05
FdEq t	9.96	9.96	- .01
Earthtone Funds:			
Ocean x	69.06	NL	- .10
Super Invest:			
MrSk r	11.73	11.73	+ .01

a. The first column indicates the fund's name. If many are listed, this is a fund family (in the example above, not all the family fund names were listed due to space limitations).

b. The second column is the Net Asset Value, or your sales price. These do not reflect deferred sales charges.

c. The third column is the Buy or Offering price, which may contain a sales charge. If there is no difference from (b) then it is no-load. Often NL will be used.

d. The fourth column designates the change from the previous day's price.

e. A "p" after the fund indicates a 12B-1 charge.

f. An "f" indicates the price is a day behind.

g. A "t" indicates both a redemption charge and a 12B-1 fee.

h. An "x" indicates the share is ex-dividend (the amount of the dividend has been deducted from the NAV and will be paid to holders of record of the fund shares).

i. An "r" after the fund indicates the price is a redemption or back-end charge.

SMART QUESTIONS TO ASK ABOUT U.S. TREASURIES

WHAT IS A TREASURY OBLIGATION?

A treasury obligation, called a Treasury Bill, Bond, or Note, is an interest-bearing obligation backed by the full faith and credit of the U.S. Treasury Department. Treasury obligations are exempt from state and local taxation.

HOW ARE THEY ISSUED?

Treasury Bills are issued in 13-week, 26-week, and 52-week maturity periods, and are issued at a discount. That means that you pay less than face value when you buy them, but you get full face value when you redeem them.

For example: A 26-week maturity period Treasury Bill could be issued at a discount for a current yield of 3.85 percent. The bill, which would mature for $10,000, would be purchased for the discount price of $9,825. The maturity value includes interest earned for the period. The amount of discount (the difference between the price paid and the amount received when the bill matures) depends on current interest rates. The lower the interest rates, the less interest is paid, and the smaller the discount. The higher the interest rates, the greater the discount.

Treasury Notes are issued in 1- to 10-year maturity periods, and Treasury Bonds are issued for longer than 10 years. Both bonds and notes pay interest every 6 months.

HOW CAN I BUY TREASURIES?

Treasury obligations can be purchased directly from the Federal Reserve Bank, through any brokerage house, and through commercial banks.

WHAT KIND OF FEES ARE INVOLVED?

Purchased directly from the Federal Reserve Bank,

there is no fee. When a broker buys them for you, you pay a commission, usually ranging anywhere from ½ percent to 3 percent of the cost of the Treasury.

WHY THEN WOULD I BUY A TREASURY OBLIGATION THROUGH A BROKER?

Although buying directly from the Federal Reserve does save a fee, most investors who purchase their Treasuries through brokers do it for convenience. Also, when you buy through a broker, you can purchase an older Treasury with a higher level of interest than new Treasury obligations may provide.

For example, although new 10-year notes may be available with 7 percent interest rates, older issues may be available at 8 percent and 8.5 percent through brokers for those who are willing to pay a premium to purchase them.

ARE THERE TAX ADVANTAGES TO INVESTMENTS IN TREASURIES?

Yes, since no state tax is due on interest earned. However, there is federal tax due.

The interest on Bills is paid at maturity and is taxable when received. The interest on Bonds and Notes is paid every six months and is taxable income as received.

WHAT ARE STRIPS?

STRIPS are zero-coupon bonds issued by the Treasury.

The term STRIPS really stands for Separate Trading Receipt of Interest and Principal Securities. STRIPS represent the interest payment from a much larger treasury bond, generally a 30-year bond. When your STRIPS come due, part of the interest from the larger bond is used to pay you the full value of your STRIPS.

This is a complicated theory to explain, but easy to understand by example. A $10,000 STRIP, maturing in ten years at 7.2 percent, would cost $5,000. In ten years when the treasury bond the STRIP came from pays its regular semiannual interest payment, part of that payment is your $10,000. These zero-coupon treasury bonds come under various acronyms: CATS (Certificates of Accrual Treasury Securities), TIGERS (Treasury Investment Growth Receipt Securities), GATORS (Government and Agency Term Obligation Receipt Securities), TRs (Treasury Receipts), ETRs (Easy Growth Treasury Receipts), CTRs (Callable Treasury Receipts or Coupon Treasury Receipts), etc. They can be excellent vehicles for retirement and college planning.

HOW ARE TREASURIES RATED?

Treasury obligations enjoy the full faith and credit of the United States Treasury Department and carry an AAA rating.

SMART QUESTIONS TO ASK ABOUT GOVERNMENT AGENCY OBLIGATIONS

WHAT IS A GOVERNMENT AGENCY OBLIGATION?

A government agency obligation refers to a certificate issued by a U.S. Government agency, such as the Federal Home Loan Mortgage Corporation. Fannie Mae's, Freddie Mac's, and Ginnie Mae's are examples of agency obligations (discussed later).

All governmental agency obligations are sold through brokers. They consist of pools of various debt obligations, of varying amounts, at various rates of interest, with various maturity dates, blended together to provide the investor with income.

HOW ARE GOVERNMENT AGENCY OBLIGATIONS RATED?

Governmental agencies are considered a moral obligation of the U.S. government and as such carry the equivalent of an AAA rating. There has never been a default of a governmental agency obligation.

I'VE HEARD YOU CAN GET HIGHER INTEREST THAN TREASURIES AND STILL GET GOVERNMENTAL GUARANTEES. WHAT KINDS OF BONDS ARE THERE?

The most commonly recognized are mortgage-backed securities. These securities are a collection of various mortgages lumped together in a "pool." The payment of interest and principal in these certificates is "passed through" directly to the investor.

It works the same as any mortgage: when you obtain a mortgage you borrow a sum of money to purchase a residence, and in return you are obligated to make monthly payments. These monthly payments are comprised of interest as well as a repayment of some of the borrowed principal. When you invest in mortgage-backed securities, you purchase the right to receive the monthly payments made by home owners on the pool of mortgages you've purchased.

You get a better than average yield from this type of investment and these bonds have triple-A ratings due to the fact that they are backed by government-owned or government-charted corporations.

WHAT IS A GINNIE MAE?

Ginnie Maes are direct obligations of the Government National Mortgage Association (GNMA, called Ginnie Mae), a government-owned corporation. Interest and principal to investors in mortgage-backed securities issued by GNMA is guaranteed by the full faith and credit of the U. S. Government.

WHAT ARE FANNIE MAEs?

Fannie Maes, as they are called, are direct obligations of the Federal National Mortgage Association (FNMA). These bonds usually carry an AAA equivalent rating.

WHAT ARE FREDDIE MACs?

Freddie Macs are direct obligations of the Federal Home Loan Mortgage Corporation, a government agency. These bonds usually carry an AAA equivalent rating.

WHY DO I GET HIGHER YIELD FROM MORTGAGE-BACKED SECURITIES THAN FROM TREASURY OBLIGATIONS?

The main reason for the higher yield is the timing of the repayment of principal to the investor. In a treasury obligation, 100 percent of the principal is repaid on the maturity date. In a mortgage-backed security, the principal is repaid over a period of years, as principal on the mortgages are paid (when a home is refinanced or sold).

With direct Treasury obligations the interest is guaranteed for the stated period with return of principal at maturity date. With mortgage obligations, return of principal cannot be predicted with complete accuracy. As the principal is repaid, the remaining or outstanding principal is guaranteed to pay the original interest rate, but the principal returned to the investor must be reinvested at existing interest rates. This uncertainty is why the investor receives additional yield.

WHAT ARE CMOs?

Collateralized Mortgage Obligations are government agency obligations of mortgage-backed securities. They can involve any of the above pools: Ginnie Mae's, Fannie Mae's, or Freddie Mac's. They are highly complex, sophisticated investments intended for income-oriented investors looking to reduce their risks.

HOW DO CMOs WORK?

The basic design of the CMO involves combining the steady, predictable income of a corporate bond (paid monthly), with the flexible repayment of principal like that of most other mortgage-backed securities discussed earlier. There are, however, significant differences. In most mortgage-backed obligations, principal is repaid every month. In CMOs, no principal is repaid until a designated period of time, called the "window," has passed. Prior to the window, only interest is paid monthly, resulting in a very predictable "stream" of income.

During the window period both interest and principal are paid, as in the more traditional mortgage-backed securities. Here is where the uncertainty comes in. When the window starts and how long it lasts is based on a series of assumptions, including how quickly people might repay their mortgages, given higher and lower interest rate scenarios. Since no assumption is guaranteed, the repayment window can start earlier and prepay faster than desired if interest rates fall. In the reverse situation, where interest rates increase, the window could start later and last longer than assumed.

If you're interested in CMOs, be sure you go to someone who really understands what happens as interest rates change.

WHAT IS A PREPAYMENT ASSUMPTION?

A prepayment assumption is used in determining the yields and the window period discussed earlier. The industry utilizes the Public Securities Association (PSA) model as a method of measurement. A higher PSA number means that interest rates are falling, people are prepaying their mortgages through refinancing, and more of the principal from your investment is coming back faster. This results in an earlier, and perhaps shorter, window period.

A smaller PSA number means that interest rates are rising, principal payments are coming back on or slower than scheduled. The end result is a later, and perhaps longer, window period.

HOW DO I KNOW IF MY BROKER IS KNOWLEDGEABLE ABOUT CMOs?

Most brokerage professionals are aware of CMOs, but buying them can be tricky. Ask the broker what happens specifically when the PSAs lengthen and shorten. For example, if a CMO is using a PSA of 150 to give you a certain window range, ask the broker when the window begins and ends at 100 PSA and at 200 PSA. The results will indicate how much fluctuation you may experience during the life of the investment. If the broker is unsure of the answers, or is unwilling to find out the answers for you, think about finding another broker.

WHERE CAN I GET MORE INFORMATION ABOUT CMOs?

Everyone who sells CMOs should have literature on them available to you which explains the terms and risks of this investment. You can also go to the library and find articles on CMOs that have recently been published in major financial periodicals such as the *Wall Street Journal* and *Money Magazine*. It's not important that you understand exactly how this type of investment works, so don't feel that you have to become an expert on the subject. You do need to understand what the risks are, and to feel comfortable making this type of investment.

SECTION 4

SMART QUESTIONS TO ASK ABOUT TAX-SAVING STRATEGIES

There are three categories of investments in this section: Municipal Bonds, Qualified Pension Accounts, and Annuities. These three categories are presented under one section title because they each offer prudent investors tax-saving strategies.

A municipal bond is a legal obligation of a village, school district, town, city, or state. The federal government encourages investors to buy these bonds by allowing interest to be earned free of federal taxes. State and local taxes are exempted as well, if you reside in the city or state that issued the bonds. These are fixed income investments, and are usually most appropriate for investors in high tax brackets.

Qualified Pension Plans are not tax free, but they are

tax deferred. These plans are designed to encourage employees of corporations, or self-employed individuals, to save for their retirement years. There are substantial penalties for withdrawing funds early, but in most cases income and capital gains are not taxed until the money is distributed. The assumption is that when you are of retirement age and ready to withdraw your money, you will be in a lower tax bracket than when you started investing. So even though you eventually do have to pay taxes, you will be paying less than if you had put this money into a nontax-deferred account.

The same theory applies to annuities. Annuities are issued through insurance companies, and are meant to provide you with a retirement income, either in a lump sum or through distributed payments. The laws governing annuities are undergoing constant change; therefore it is of utmost importance that you consult your accountant, insurance agent, and/or financial advisor before making this a personal investment choice.

SMART QUESTIONS TO ASK ABOUT MUNICIPAL BONDS

HOW DOES A MUNICIPALITY SELL BONDS?

First of all, the municipality needs permission from the public to issue bonds. These are the issues you often see on election ballots. When that permission is given (meaning that the ballot is passed by the voting public), the municipality finds a bank or institution of finance to be the issuing agency. At the maturity date (or at the callable date), the bonds are redeemed. The municipality can pay off its obligation by issuing new bonds and using the proceeds to pay off the old bonds, or by using money from surplus tax revenues.

HOW CAN AN INDIVIDUAL BUY A MUNICIPAL BOND?

Municipal bonds can be purchased in the same manner as other bonds sold through brokerage houses and banks. New issues (bonds) are advertised by their underwriters who publish a list of brokerage houses that have these bonds available for sale. All bonds are traded on the various exchanges daily.

IS THERE A MINIMUM AMOUNT REQUIRED TO INVEST IN MUNICIPAL BONDS?

If you are buying an individual bond you should think in terms of an investment of $25,000 or more. When these bonds are purchased in lower denominations, the cost to the purchaser is greater, and when they have to be sold, the cost to the seller is greater. This means a lower overall yield to the investor.

SUPPOSE I ONLY HAVE $1,000. CAN I GET INTO INVESTMENTS IN MUNICIPAL BONDS?

Yes. There are municipal bond mutual funds available which allow you to invest with as little as $1,000. The advantage of a mutual fund is that you can often add as little as $50 at a time to purchase more shares.

Municipal bond funds are usually open ended; new money invested in the fund will be used to purchase bonds currently being offered. That means there will be a wide variety of interest rates and maturity dates in your fund.

The biggest advantage of municipal bond funds is guaranteed liquidity, which means you can sell your shares whenever you need to and get your cash quickly.

HOW DO I KNOW WHEN TO SELL TO AVOID A LOSS?

If you wish to sell without incurring a loss, you must keep good records of the cost of your shares, and be aware of the fluctuations of interest rates. The price per share in a bond fund is directly related to current interest rates. When interest rates go down, price per share will rise. Conversely, when rates go up, price per share will go down. If you keep records of your investment and reinvestment amounts, it will be easy to determine your profit or loss potential.

I DON'T REALLY WANT TO MAKE A LONG-TERM INVESTMENT. SHOULD I CONSIDER SHORT-TERM MUNICIPAL BONDS?

The yield you will get from investment in a municipal bond depends on the bond's maturity date. Historically, the shorter the time to the maturity date the lower the interest rate. However, interest rates don't always follow historical patterns. For example, there was a period of time in the early 1980s where short-term rates were actually higher than long-term rates.

HOW DO YOU DEFINE SHORT OR LONG TERM?

A short-term bond is one that matures in less than 10 years. An intermediate term bond is one that will mature sometime between 10 and 20 years. Long-term bonds can run as long as 30 to 40 years. For that reason you must be very clear about your objective when you purchase bonds. If income is your primary purpose then buying long term should be your choice. If, however, you want to "park" your money in a tax-free environment for a short period of time, a tax-free money market bond fund might be a good bet. These funds invests in very short (thirty to ninety day) tax-free instruments such as Bond Anticipation Notes (BANs), Revenue Anticipation Notes (RANs), and Tax Anticipation Notes (TANs).

WHAT OTHER WAYS ARE THERE TO GET INVOLVED IN TAX-FREE BONDS?

Aside from single issue bonds, tax-free money markets, short-term, intermediate, and long-term mutual bond funds, you can purchase municipal bond trusts. These combine and blend many different issues and rates. The difference between a trust and a fund is that the trust is finite (comes to an end) and will ultimately pay out all principal invested. Bond trusts can be purchased in intermediate and long-term issues and also can be purchased insured as to payment of interest and repayment of principal.

THE MUNICIPALITY IN WHICH I LIVE (AND FROM WHICH I BUY BONDS) IS HAVING MAJOR BUDGET PROBLEMS. HOW DO I KNOW THE MUNICIPALITY WON'T GO BANKRUPT AND MAKE MY BONDS WORTHLESS?

You can purchase insured municipal bond portfolios which guarantee payment of interest and principal on time. That will usually cost you anywhere from ¼ to ½ of a percent in terms of the income you will get from those bonds. For instance, if an uninsured bond yields 7 percent, an insured bond may yield 6.6 percent. However, the extra cost may be worth it to you to know that your investment price includes insurance.

ARE STATE TAX-FREE BOND FUNDS RISK-FREE?

No. Most state tax-free bond funds are uninsured and do carry a degree of risk. There are insured state funds using private insurance companies to insure return of principal. Only large capitalization insurance companies generally insure municipal bonds. Municipal Bond Assurance Corporation (AMBAC) issues the majority of insured bonds.

When you buy a state fund (a federal and state tax-free investment to state residents) you limit the diversification of bonds and geographic area to the portfolio. This limitation adds additional risk to the portfolio. When choosing a state fund, include the additional risk of reduced diversification (especially if you live in a small state) in your decision.

HOW DO I KNOW IF TAX-FREE BONDS ARE GOOD FOR ME?

Since tax-free bonds offer lower interest than taxable ones, you have to know whether or not they are a good deal for you. In order to answer this question, you must review your entire financial picture, placing particular emphasis on your tax bracket. Sometimes it makes more sense to take the higher yield that a taxable bond would give you (the taxable equivalent yield) because after you pay your taxes you still net more than is currently available in tax-free bonds.

Here's how it works: Suppose you invest $10,000. For someone in a 28 percent tax bracket, a 6 percent tax-free yield on $10,000 is the equivalent of an 8.33 percent taxable yield. The tax-free 6 percent yield would give you $600. An 8.33 percent taxable yield would give you $833, from which you then subtract your 28 percent (approximately $233) in taxes. The figure you arrive at would be the same $600:

$$6\% \times \$10,000 = \$600.00 \qquad \begin{array}{r} 8.33\% \times \$10,000 = \$833.00 \\ -\ 28\% \text{ taxes} = \underline{233.00} \\ \text{Total yield} = \$600.00 \end{array}$$

If you are in a higher tax bracket, say 38 percent, you would have to subtract 38 percent of $833, or $316.54. That would leave you with a yield of only $516.46:

$$6\% \times \$10,000 = \$600.00 \qquad \begin{array}{r} 8.33\% \times \$10,000 = \$833.00 \\ -\ 38\% \text{ taxes} = \underline{316.54} \\ \text{Total yield} = \$516.46 \end{array}$$

Obviously then, the higher your tax bracket, the more advantageous are tax-free bonds. If you need help figuring your net yield equivalent, your broker or your accountant would be happy to help you.

IS THERE A FORMULA TO DETERMINE THE TAXABLE EQUIVALENT YIELD?

Yes there is, and it is as follows: Divide the tax-free yield by 100 percent minus your total tax bracket, and that will give you the taxable equivalent yield.

The formula looks like this:

$$\frac{\text{Tax free Yield}}{\text{100\% - Total Tax Bracket}} = \text{Taxable Equivalent Yield}$$

Using the example above of a 6 percent yield and a 28 percent tax bracket (subtracting 28 percent from 100 percent gives you 72 percent, or .72), the formula would look like:

$$\frac{6}{.72} = 8.33\%$$

If you were in the higher tax bracket of 38 percent, the formula would be:

$$\frac{6}{.62} = 9.76\%$$

Suppose you were considering buying two bonds, one tax-free yielding 6 percent and one taxable yielding 8.33 percent. If you were in the 28 percent tax bracket, you could choose either one and get the same yield. But if you were in the higher tax bracket, you'd have to find a bond yielding at least 9.67 percent to get the same yield, so you'd be better off choosing the tax-free bond.

WHAT IS THE RISK IN INVESTING IN MUNICIPAL BONDS?

The greatest risk is the possibility of default. No municipal fund or trust, no matter how high in quality, has the security of federal deposit insurance or guarantees.

Municipal bonds are affected by changes in interest rates. Like all bonds, their value increases when interest rates decline and falls when interest rates increase. In other words, if you buy a tax-free bond with an interest rate of 6 percent, and market rates generally rise to 8 percent, your bond will decrease in value. Conversely, if you buy when interest rates are at 8 percent, and the market subsequently falls to 6 percent, your bond will increase in value.

Also, if you have made a profit when you sell your investment, it is subject to full capital gains taxation.

WHAT IS THE GREATEST ADVANTAGE OF THESE TAX-FREE INVESTMENTS?

The greatest advantage is their tax-free status, especially for those people in higher tax brackets. Since bonds are rated (so you can get an idea of their quality before you make a purchase) and can also be purchased insured, they are considered desirable as income generators.

WHAT IS THE GREATEST DISADVANTAGE OF THIS TYPE OF INVESTMENT?

The greatest disadvantage in this type of investment, and any others that are fixed in nature (the interest rate remains the same over the life of the investment), is the lack of growth available. Because of inflation, these investments produce income which buys less and less over time, and returns capital which has less buying power at maturity.

WHAT IS A GENERAL OBLIGATION BOND?

General obligation bonds, the largest category of municipal bonds, are secured by the full taxing ability of the municipality issuing them. For example, principal and interest on general obligation bonds of a local government are usually paid out of a general fund supplied by taxes levied on all taxable property within that governing area. These bonds are normally considered to offer a high level of security for the investor.

WHAT ARE REVENUE BONDS?

Revenue bonds are issued to finance many different kinds of projects, such as oil, gas, or electric facilities, hospitals, dormitories, stadiums, electric power projects, bridges, tunnels, and turnpikes. The principal and interest on these bonds are payable only from the revenues produced by the project.

For example, Turnpike Authority Bonds are paid off out of the net earning from tolls produced by those roads. These bonds are particularly attractive to the income-oriented investor, and are not considered particularly risky.

WHAT ARE HOUSING AUTHORITY BONDS?

These are usually issued to finance the construction of low rent housing projects and are secured by the Housing Assistance Administration (HFA), which is a federal agency. These bonds are considered very high quality.

WHAT ARE INDUSTRIAL DEVELOPMENT BONDS?

IDBs, as they are called, are issued by a municipality but payments are made by the industrial corporations that use or occupy the facilities that were built by the bond issue.

HOW DO I FIND OUT HOW A BOND IS RATED?

Bond ratings are made available to the public and are published by various agencies. The information is public and available to anyone seeking it. If you are interested in a particular bond which is just coming to market it would usually have the Standard & Poor's or Moody's rating in the announcement of the issue. The issue announcements can be found in the *Wall Street Journal* and most major newspapers. These ratings are subject to changes periodically and the changes are also published.

SUPPOSE I BUY A BOND THAT IS RATED A. WILL IT STAY RATED A UNTIL MATURITY?

Not necessarily. As many municipal bond investors have learned, there have been bonds that were rated A when they were issued, but were downgraded because of a reanalysis of the municipality's ability to pay interest and repay the principal at maturity. As stated earlier, municipal bonds are backed by the full faith and credit of the municipality (except for special tax bonds), and carry the risk of taxing power by the municipality. In the most severe cases, principal invested may not be completely returned. There have, however, historically been very few defaults in the municipal bond area.

MY FRIEND IS PAYING A TAX ON HIS MUNICIPAL BOND BECAUSE HE FALLS IN THE "ALTERNATIVE MINIMUM TAX BRACKET." WHAT DOES THAT MEAN?

While the interest on most municipal bonds is free of regular federal income tax, the interest on certain private activity bonds issued after August 7, 1986 is considered to be taxable. The interest on those bonds could potentially be subject to a 21 percent alternative minimum tax. Be sure to ask your broker to find out if any bonds in which you are interested fall into this category.

DO YOU MEAN THAT EVEN THOUGH I BUY TAX-FREE BONDS I COULD HAVE TO PAY TAX?

Yes, but only for certain agency issues. Therefore, you should be very careful when buying tax-frees to avoid any issues which would subject you to alternative minimum tax. Consult your accountant.

SMART QUESTIONS TO ASK ABOUT QUALIFIED PENSION ACCOUNTS

WHAT IS A QUALIFIED PENSION ACCOUNT?

A pension account is generally one to which you or the company you work for contributes money regularly. The funds which accumulate are intended to be the basis or source of income for your retirement years.

Most of the pension or profit sharing plans of corporations are contributed to entirely by the corporations. Self-employed individuals are permitted to set up their own plans as are individuals who do not participate in any other plans.

HOW IS A PENSION PLAN A TAX-SAVING STRATEGY?

The dollars contributed to a pension plan are free of any taxation until withdrawal. An added tax benefit comes from the fact that any income which accrues in the account during the accumulation phase is also free of any current taxation.

For example, a self-employed individual can contribute as much as $30,000 to a Keogh plan (see page 155) from his or her annual income. The immediate tax saving in a 28 percent bracket is $8,400. That means that the $30,000 contribution actually cost $21,600 since without the contribution plan, $8,400 would have gone to the Internal Revenue Service.

WHAT DOES THE TERM "QUALIFIED" MEAN IN A PENSION PLAN ACCOUNT?

The term qualified means that the IRS has approved the plan for contributions to a retirement savings account for an individual. These contributions "qualify" for exemption from current taxation for the contributor. Typical plans include Money-Purchase, Profit Sharing, Defined Benefit, Keogh, SEP, 401K, 403B, and IRA accounts (descriptions follow later in this section).

DO I REALLY NEED A RETIREMENT PLAN?

With inflation the way it is, and with life expectancy steadily increasing, putting money away for your retirement is no longer an option—it is a necessity. It would be wonderful if we all could earn huge amounts of money, and have the incentive and willpower to save enough of it to carry us through our "golden years." Unfortunately, not everyone earns a fortune—and even those who do often have trouble saving any of it. This is where pension plans come in.

You could compare a pension plan to earning residuals for work already accomplished. When an actor appears in a TV commercial, he is paid a certain amount for his work. Thereafter, every time that commercial is shown again, he receives a residual, or payment, for the work that was done in the past. When you work for a company, you earn a salary for the work that you do. When the company contributes to your pension plan, it is putting away money toward paying you residuals for the work you contributed in the past. If you are self-employed, you must pay yourself your own residuals, so you must set up your own pension plan.

CAN I USE A RETIREMENT PLAN AS A TAX-PLANNING STRATEGY?

From a tax perspective, retirement planning can be the most important planning an investor can use to save money, since no current taxes are withdrawn from the money. With few exceptions, all money contributed to the plan goes on deposit free of federal, state, or city taxes. In addition, all interest or capital gains earned by the investment are also free of taxation until withdrawn.

WHO IS THE BEST PERSON TO ADVISE ME ABOUT SETTING UP A PENSION PLAN?

Probably the person who knows your financial picture best is your accountant. She can guide you as to setting up your own plans based on your current cash flow and tax bracket. A certified financial planner who is thoroughly familiar with your financial situation can usually be of help in designing an appropriate plan as well.

ARE INSURANCE AGENTS KNOWLEDGEABLE ABOUT PENSION PLANS?

Many agents are knowledgeable, but are restricted to those plans made available through insurance companies.

ARE CONTRIBUTIONS TO A RETIREMENT PLAN TAX DEDUCTIBLE?

They are tax deductible to whomever makes the contribution. For example, if the company you work for contributes on your behalf it is a deduction for the corporation. If, however, you (as the employee) make the contribution to the plan, then it is a deduction for you.

HOW IS IT DETERMINED WHO MAKES THE CONTRIBUTION—YOU OR THE COMPANY YOU WORK FOR?

If a corporation, municipality, or other employer has a pension plan, they usually make the entire contribution. Some plans allow for supplemental contributions of up to 10 percent of salary by the employee as well. If you are self-employed, of course you make all the contributions yourself.

WHAT ARE THE RESTRICTIONS OF QUALIFIED RETIREMENT PLANS?

Each type of plan has its own restrictions, particularly with respect to how much money you can contribute. Other restrictions have to do with taking money out of the plan before you reach age 59 ½ (except for death, disability, and early retirement). Not only are early distributions taxable, but a penalty excise tax of 10 percent of the distribution is also levied.

Distributions must begin by April 15th of the year following the year in which you reach age 70½. Otherwise, a 50 percent penalty tax is imposed on the amount by which the distribution fails to meet the minimum distribution requirement (set up by a lifetime actuarial schedule issued by the IRS). For example, if the minimum is $3,200 and the distribution taken is $2,000, the extra penalty is $600.

HOW DO I GET MONEY OUT OF THE PLAN?

There are several ways to remove money from a qualified retirement plan. Rollovers, transfers, lump-sum distributions, 5-year payouts, and lifetime annuitization (monthly checks for life) are all ways to move and remove money in a retirement plan. A better description and the tax impact of each strategy is discussed later in this section.

ARE FUNDS FROM THESE PLANS EVER AVAILABLE TO ME BEFORE I RETIRE?

Some plans do permit loans before retirement for very specific reasons, most commonly medical emergencies, first home purchase, and education. Other plans allow unrestricted loans which must be repaid within five years.

SUPPOSE I LEAVE MY JOB FOR ANOTHER ONE? DO I HAVE ANY RIGHTS TO THE MONEY WHICH HAS BEEN ACCUMULATED FOR MY BENEFIT?

That usually depends on how long you've worked for the company. You may not be entitled to participate in the pension plan at all until you've worked there for a number of months, or even years. And all plans wholly funded by the employer have "vesting" schedules—in other words, the percentage of funds to which you are entitled increases with the length of time you've been with the firm.

However, any funds you have personally contributed to any retirement plan are 100 percent vested immediately, and you have the right to remove those funds.

SUPPOSE I AM "ENCOURAGED" TO LEAVE MY JOB AT AGE 55. WHAT PROTECTION DO I HAVE IF I HAVE NOT BEEN THERE LONG ENOUGH TO BE FULLY VESTED, AND NEED TO HAVE INCOME?

In most recent cases, firms trying to eliminate jobs by giving attractive termination packages to employees have agreed to honor a 100 percent vesting of the funds set aside for that employee.

HOW WILL I KNOW WHAT'S IN MY PENSION PLAN?

Most large companies issue quarterly or semiannual statements which reflect contributions made on your behalf to your account. Many smaller companies issue annual statements only.

WHAT PAPERS SHOULD I KEEP?

By federal regulation, all plans must distribute plan documents to participants. Keep all statements that reflect contributions and investment performance, and any that show beneficiary designations.

WHAT HAPPENS WHEN A QUALIFIED PLAN IS TERMINATED? WHAT PROTECTION DO I HAVE?

This is a particularly relevant question since so many companies have discontinued their plans or have stopped making contributions. Under federal regulation, plan contributions are protected by vesting schedules and rights at termination. However, there is no guarantee of distribution if the plan is merely frozen or if contributions have stopped. If termination occurs, the plan must distribute assets on a prorata basis to all participants based on their account balances.

WHAT KINDS OF RETIREMENT PLANS ARE THERE?

There are basically two types of plans which you, as a self-employed individual or as an employee of a larger corporation have available. The first is a defined contribution plan, and the second is a defined benefit plan.

WHAT IS A DEFINED CONTRIBUTION PLAN?

A defined contribution plan allows a maximum contribution of 25 percent of net earned income or $30,000, whichever is less. Two common types of defined contribution plans are Money Purchase and Profit Sharing plans.

WHAT IS A MONEY PURCHASE PLAN?

Contributions to money purchase plans *must* be made annually (by a company for its employees) regardless of the company's profit or loss. The amount of money a company must contribute is a predetermined percentage of the payroll. Contributions are limited to a maximum of 25 percent of an employee's salary, up to $30,000 per individual. The amount of monthly income an individual receives at retirement is not predetermined, as it is in a defined benefit plan (discussed later). The income depends on the quantity of regular contributions and the performance of the investments related to the fund. The more money that is contributed and/or the better the investment performance, the more income at retirement.

HOW IS A MONEY PURCHASE PLAN DESIGNED?

A money purchase plan can be specifically designed and tailored for you by an actuary and a plan administrator, or you can use a preapproved plan called a "prototype." The prototype plan has preapproved qualification requirements and rules. Most brokerage houses and mutual funds have prototypes available. In general, prototypes provide most of what you desire in a plan at a more reasonable cost.

WHAT IS A PROFIT-SHARING PLAN?

Profit-sharing plans are the most frequently used since no contribution must be made by the company if there are no excess profits. No contribution is mandatory; therefore, employers find this plan most flexible. For example, it is not unusual for a young company to have good intentions about funding plans for their employees. However, in a year when revenues decrease, or investment in new equipment causes expenses to increase, the company has no obligation to make contributions to the plan.

This type of plan is much more advantageous to the employer than it is to the employee. The employer may never make any contributions, but as long as there is a plan in effect, the employee cannot open an Individual Retirement Account.

WHAT ARE DEFINED BENEFIT PLANS?

A defined benefit plan specifies how much monthly income will be received upon retirement. The amount of income depends on retirement age and salary in the five years preceding retirement. The exact percentage is an actuarial calculation.

Unlike the defined contribution plan, the contribution varies based on the age of the participants and the investment performance. The better the investment performance, the smaller the contribution, not the larger the benefit. This is the major difference between the two types of plans. These contributions are made at a reasonable time after the completion of the company's fiscal year, and are tax deductible to the company.

All benefits to eligible employees are nondiscriminatory. That means all eligible participants of the plan are subject to the same formulas and rules in determining the amount of monthly retirement income. The amount of income will be different, just as the current salaries are; however, the determination of the benefit will be calculated using the same formula.

WHAT IS AN IRA?

An IRA, or Individual Retirement Account, allows individuals with no other pension plan to invest up to $2,000 per year in a retirement account, and deduct that amount from taxable income. There are some restrictions, however, on the deductibility of $2,000 from income; check with your tax advisor to find out if restrictions apply to your specific situation. IRAs are governed by the same rules as other qualified plans in regard to distribution regulations.

I HEARD YOU CAN PUT MONEY IN AN IRA AND NOT DEDUCT IT FROM YOUR TAXABLE INCOME. DOES THAT MAKE SENSE?

There are many who suggest the use of an IRA account even when it is not deductible from taxable income, since it will still earn tax-deferred interest. However, since currently you can have the same advantage by using a tax-deferred annuity or a savings bond as an investment vehicle, there is no real advantage to it.

WHAT IS THE DIFFERENCE BETWEEN AN IRA AND AN IRA ROLLOVER?

A rollover is the investment of funds obtained by termination of employment from any qualified plan, or from an IRA investment which matures. You have the use of these funds for sixty days from the date of withdrawal before you have to make a new IRA contribution. If you have not rolled over the funds after 60 days, you incur tax penalties, and if you are under age 59½, you will incur an added penalty tax of 10 percent as well.

I HAVE MONEY IN A BANK IRA CD. CAN I MOVE THIS TO A MUTUAL FUND?

It is possible to remove funds from one IRA account to another, either by rollover, as described above, or direct bank-to-bank transfer. For example, you have an IRA investment in a bank CD. At maturity (although you do not have to wait until maturity), you wish to move this money to a mutual fund. You must do this within 60 days of withdrawing the money in order to avoid taxation and penalty.

If you do not want to take physical possession of the money but still wish to move it to a mutual fund, you can transfer it.

For example, you have an IRA at a bank and currently have accumulated $12,000 there. You now want to invest that money in a mutual fund. You apply to the bank custodian for IRA accounts at the mutual fund company to accept a transfer of money from your bank. You then also make application to your bank to transfer the money.

When your bank receives the transfer papers along with the acceptance of transfer signed by the new custodian of your IRA account, the funds will be transferred on a "bank-to-bank" transfer.

ARE THERE OTHER PLACES TO WHICH I CAN TRANSFER THESE FUNDS?

You are not limited to banks and mutual funds. Brokerage accounts offer IRAs and other retirement plans for investment diversification. Also, there are trust companies, similar to banks, that specialize in retirement plans that offer more flexibility than other options. They are generally more expensive, so the cost of flexibility should be included in your decision about where to place your money. Remember, you don't have to keep all your money in one place—there is nothing wrong with having money in two or more of these options.

WHAT IS A KEOGH?

A Keogh plan allows a self-employed individual or small business to set up retirement accounts for all full-time employees. It can be money purchase only or profit-sharing only or a combination of both. The maximum contributions are limited to $30,000. However, a defined benefit Keogh can allow for much larger contributions.

WHAT ARE THE DISADVANTAGES OF A KEOGH?

If the plan is only intended to provide profit sharing, there are administrative and tax preparation costs involved with a Keogh that make other plans much more attractive.

WHAT IS A SEP?

A Simplified Employee Pension (SEP) Plan is another way funds can be set aside by employers. A SEP is limited to 15 percent of gross income, to a maximum of $30,000 per year. It is intended for small businesses (defined as those with ten or fewer participants). The employer-funded SEP allows the employer to make tax-deductible contributions on behalf of the employee. A SEP combines the advantages of a qualified plan, but is as simple as an IRA.

Qualifying employers also offer salary deduction plans which allow employees to contribute an annually adjusted-for-inflation amount of pretax wages to their SEPs. This contribution reduces the employee's taxable salary and is not subject to taxation until it is distributed to the employee.

WHAT IS A 401K?

The 401K is a tax-sheltered retirement plan designed for use by corporate employers as a benefit to their employees. This plan provides, through salary reduction agreements, the ability of individual corporate employees to contribute, pretax, up to 15 percent of their salary. The maximum permitted as a contribution changes annually.

Your 401K contribution is not counted as part of your

gross income. Your W-2 form for reporting income will not include it. Therefore, all contributions effectively provide a tax deduction. An added benefit is that all of the plans' earnings are also tax deferred. In addition, the employer may match deposits to a given stated percentage, usually from 3 to 6 percent of your gross income.

ARE 401K PLANS GOVERNMENT REGULATED AS WELL?

Yes. Historically, most qualified pension plans were designed to benefit the upper management. Since the contributions were usually based on a percentage of salary, those with a larger salary got a greater reward. However, government regulations now prescribe that a minimum number of lower-salaried employees must participate for the plan to be deemed "qualified" for exemption from current taxation. The matching contribution made by the employer is intended as an incentive for every employee to participate in the plan. The plan must follow government guidelines to prevent the employees at the top of the salary schedule from benefiting to a greater extent than the balance of the employees.

WHAT IS A 403B?

The tax-sheltered 403B is a plan designed for nonprofit entities. Each participant is limited to deposits of $9,500 per year. Participants may make contributions of up to $12,500 per year for the three years prior to retirement if they have not consistently made contributions to the plan throughout their work life. This is known as the "catch up" provision. Investments in 403Bs are limited to annuities and mutual funds.

WHAT IS A LUMP SUM DISTRIBUTION?

Lump sum distribution means that you receive all the money in your retirement plan at once within one year of its termination. This sum is reported to you on form 1099-R. They are the result of funds that you or your employer accumulated in any of the above retirement plans. In other words, the funds can come from a corporate defined benefit or defined contribution plan, a Keogh, a SEP, a 401K, or a 403B. All of these plans cease upon the termination of employment, whether because of retirement, job change, or job termination.

WILL I ALWAYS RECEIVE A LUMP SUM DISTRIBUTION OF MY QUALIFIED PENSION ACCOUNT?

Employers must distribute the vested amount in most plans. For example, a 401K which has always been 100 percent vested, or owned, by the employee must be distributed. Any investments which can be converted to cash will be distributed as cash. If there are shares of stocks involved, they can be distributed in a stock certificate. All of this is eligible for rollover.

If you are less than 100 percent vested in the plan, the employer is only obligated to distribute the vested portion as a lump sum.

In the case of a defined benefit plan which is still active, you may have the option of a lump sum or you may be asked to select a lifetime annuity or designated payment period as a distribution option.

HOW MUCH OF MY LUMP SUM WILL BE TAXABLE TO ME?

In general, all of the lump sum will be taxable. This includes the employer contributions, employee pretax contributions, and all the earnings in the account. Employee pretax contributions include payroll deductions made prior to taxation and contributed to the plan.

Some plans allow for employees to contribute into the plan with after-tax payroll. This is sometimes referred to as a tax-deferred savings plan. The earnings on these contributions are subject to tax on a lump sum distribution; however, the employee after-tax contribution is not taxed again. The lump sum, except for employee after-tax contributions, is eligible for IRA rollover.

I REALLY WANT TO ROLL EVERYTHING OVER SINCE I DON'T WANT TO DISTURB MY RETIREMENT FUNDS. WHY CAN'T I DO THAT?

The result of rolling over an after-tax contribution will be double taxation. You paid tax before you made the contribution and will now pay tax when you withdraw it. Seek professional advice before you roll over any lump sum distribution.

WHEN DOES PENSION PLAN MONEY BECOME TAXABLE?

None of the qualified pension plans will produce taxable income until you start receiving payments. For example, if you have an IRA rollover account in a mutual fund, you can continue to earn dividends, interest, and capital gains without current taxation. Let's assume that at age 65, you will want to supplement your Social Security and/or pension check with additional income. You can direct the mutual fund company to send you a specified amount monthly, or a lump sum amount, at any time. The amounts received will be taxable but the balance of the account will continue to earn income that is not taxed.

I'M ONLY 55. WILL I HAVE TO PAY A PENALTY IF I TAKE PART OF MY RETIREMENT DISTRIBUTION?

If you have been terminated or retired from employment there will be no penalty for accepting all or any part of the lump sum distribution. Once the funds are taxed at regular income tax rates, there will be no further taxation due on that lump sum. However, if you are under 59½ when you receive the payment it makes more sense for the funds to remain tax deferred by rolling the distribution into an IRA within 60 days of receipt. This will allow your pension benefits to continue to grow tax-deferred until you need them in retirement.

I'VE HEARD THAT I CAN USE A FIVE-YEAR AVERAGING FORMULA. WHAT IS IT, AND HOW DO I KNOW IF I SHOULD USE THE AVERAGING FORMULA OR NOT?

If you are over 59½ when you receive the distribution you can use a special five-year averaging formula that treats the funds as though they were received over a five-year period. Even though the entire distribution is taxed in the year you receive it, the tax rate for these funds is much lower than the normal income tax rate. Any recipient who turned age 50 before 1986 may be eligible for 10-year averaging. That averaging formula is based on 1986 income tax rates. The five-year averaging formula uses current year rates.

HOW WILL I KNOW IF I AM REMOVING MY QUALIFIED RETIREMENT PENSION MONEY IN THE RIGHT AMOUNTS AND AT THE RIGHT TIME?

It is best to have your accountant do a five-year projection or "look-ahead" at your income. If the total sum of your qualified pension accounts exceed one million dollars, you can run into excess distributions (see page 162) unless you select a payout option which will allow you to project your life expectancy with someone younger. Married couples, for example, are permitted to assume a joint and survivor, or two-lives, payout option. If you want to be sure this deferred income becomes taxable in the best way and at the best rates, you should get a professional to give you advice.

I'M 62 NOW AND RETIRED. I FEEL I HAVE ENOUGH INCOME FOR THE TIME BEING. MUST I START TAKING MONEY OUT OF MY RETIREMENT ACCOUNTS?

Accounts you have established yourself, such as IRA and IRA rollover accounts, need not be distributed to you until age 70½. You may withdraw any or all of your IRA at any time between ages 59½ and 70½ without penalty.

I HAVE NOW REACHED THE WONDERFUL AGE OF 70½. DO I HAVE TO TAKE ALL MY MONEY OUT OF MY RETIREMENT ACCOUNTS?

You must begin withdrawals by April 15 of the year following the year in which you reach age 70½. Thereafter distributions must be made by December 31 of each year. The amount of the payment is determined by actuarial tables set up by the IRS which measure your life expectancy. Failure to take at least the minimum distribution triggers a 50 percent penalty tax on the difference between the minimum required payment and the actual payment.

WHAT ARE EXCESS DISTRIBUTIONS?

If you have no current need for the income, the temptation is to allow retirement accounts to accumulate. Under the Tax Reform Act of 1986, however, distributions each year cannot exceed certain limits or a 15 percent additional excise tax is levied on the amount over the permitted limit. Just as the IRS has determined minimum levels, it has also determined maximum ones. This applies to both defined benefit and defined contribution plans. Be sure when you turn 65 or 66 you have a tax advisor determine whether or not you should begin distributions so that the amount which will be in your account at age 70½ does not create excessive distribution problems.

WHAT HAPPENS TO THESE RETIREMENT FUNDS WHEN I DIE? WHO PAYS THE TAXES THEN?

If you die before distributions begin, your beneficiary has rights to the accumulated funds. If you have a spouse, your account can be moved to an IRA rollover account in the spouse's name without any tax consequences. If, however, you have no spouse, distribution may take two forms. The first is equal distribution over a five-year period fully taxable to the recipient in his or her tax bracket. The second is a monthly annuity distribution to the beneficiary which will be taxable as received.

If you die after the start of distributions, taxation will depend on the manner in which distributions have begun. If the funds have been converted to a pension, then the payout option you chose will determine tax consequences. For example, if you have converted your IRA account to a pension which will pay for life but for 20 years certain and you die in year seven, your beneficiary will continue to receive your pension for the thirteen years which remain in the certain period. There are many variables involved in this procedure, and you will need to discuss possible consequences with your financial advisor when you choose a payout plan for your funds.

HOW DO I DECIDE WHICH WITHDRAWAL OPTIONS MAKE THE MOST SENSE FOR ME?

Since this is such a complicated—and vitally important—subject, most people need the help of an accountant or financial planner in determining the most tax-effective way to take distributions. Much depends on your total financial picture. How much to take, when to take it, and in what form can be best decided only after a detailed analysis of your assets and liabilities and your current and potential sources of income has been completed.

SMART QUESTIONS TO ASK ABOUT ANNUITIES

WHAT IS AN ANNUITY?

An annuity is an investment vehicle issued by an insurance company. Instead of paying a death benefit to your beneficiaries, an annuity pays you a monetary benefit during your lifetime. It also allows you to save on a tax-deferred basis.

The investment used can be "fixed." For example, you can purchase an annuity with a guaranteed rate of 6 percent interest for one year. Or the investment used can be "variable," involving a mutual fund variety of bond and stock investments.

An annuity can be an important instrument in planning for retirement. By generic description, an annuity provides lifetime income. It is a way of turning cash into a guaranteed income stream. You pay in premiums over time, or all at once. Finally, when you need the money for retirement, one of the contract's options is to guarantee a specific monthly payment for as long as you or your spouse lives. If you die before payments begin, your beneficiaries receive the accumulated funds. If you die after payments begin, beneficiaries receive payments according to the type of annuity you have and the payment options of that annuity.

IS AN ANNUITY A GOOD INVESTMENT?

Annuities can provide an excellent opportunity for deferral of current taxation on earnings. This means that there are no taxes due on interest, dividends, or capital gains earned in the account while it remains in an accumulation period. Once the annuity begins paying out money, taxes are then due.

WHERE CAN I GET AN ANNUITY?

You can buy them only from insurance companies that issue annuities through their agents.

HOW DO I CHOOSE AN INSURANCE COMPANY THROUGH WHICH TO PURCHASE AN ANNUITY?

It is more important than ever to do your own research and utilize caution when choosing an insurance company. Although the insurance industry is strong overall, the recession hurt many of their investments. Only deal with insurance companies who have been rated well by Best & Co., Duff & Phelps, Standard and Poor's, and Moody's. Choosing an insurance company which is well rated and whose variable funds have good track records could require professional guidance.

I HAVE JUST PURCHASED AN ANNUITY. WHAT WILL I RECEIVE FROM THE INSURANCE COMPANY?

You will receive a life insurance annuity contract not unlike, in appearance, a life insurance policy. It will name the annuitant (the person who receives the payments), the beneficiaries, and the owner of the contract (who may or may not be the same as the annuitant). It is the owner who controls the contract and can make changes; for example, the owner can change the beneficiaries.

HOW DOES AN ANNUITY DIFFER FROM A PENSION PLAN INVESTMENT?

Most pension plans have "qualified" dollars invested. In other words, all sums invested (through a payroll deduction plan, pension or profit sharing or any of a variety of self-employment plans like SEP or Keogh) are removed from current taxation. In those accounts, earnings also enjoy the benefits of tax deferral.

In an annuity purchased with "regular," or nonqualified dollars, taxes have been paid on the investment sums, but earnings enjoy the benefit of tax deferral.

WHAT KINDS OF ANNUITIES ARE AVAILABLE?

There are four basic types of annuities:

Fixed Annuity: generally refers to an annuity that pays a specified rate of interest, usually set by the insurance company once a year, with a guarantee of principal. In that it guarantees a certain rate of return for a specific period of time, an annuity is very similar to a bond. For example, you can invest $10,000 and receive a guarantee of 6 percent for one year. At renewal date, a new one-year rate will be given and guaranteed for the next year. Annuities are also available with fixed rates for three, five, seven, and ten years.

Variable Annuity: generally refers to an annuity that neither guarantees principal nor interest, but allows for a greater rate of return than a fixed annuity. But, buyer beware: just as it is possible for the annuity to increase in value, it is also possible for the annuity to *decrease* in value.

A variable annuity allows for investment in a variety of mutual funds. These can include money markets, government securities, stocks, and global investments. Some companies offer variable annuities that guarantee principal on death. For example: If you invested $10,000 in a variable annuity and the annuitant (yourself) died, your beneficiary would receive $10,000 or the market value of the annuity, whichever was higher.

Immediate Annuity: can be either a fixed or variable annuity that immediately begins paying benefits to the annuitant. This would typically be bought by a person who has reached retirement and wants to begin receiving monthly payments.

Deferred Annuity: can be either a fixed or variable annuity that isn't expected to pay benefits until some future point in time. This annuity would typically be bought by a younger person interested in saving for retirement.

WHAT IS THE PRINCIPAL ADVANTAGE IN INVESTING IN A DEFERRED ANNUITY?

The principal advantage is in tax savings. Money that is earning you interest without being taxed is a better investment than money that is being taxed annually. An annuity has no tax consequence until you remove the funds.

For example, a $10,000 investment can earn interest and/or capital gains and it all grows without current taxation until money is withdrawn. In a Fixed Return Annuity, $10,000 could grow to $19,672 in 10 years at 7 percent. If you had paid taxes on the interest at a 28 percent rate annually you would have ended up with $16,351. If, after 10 years, you withdraw the entire $19,672 from the annuity, you will have to pay taxes on your earnings ($9,672) all in one tax year. At the same 28 percent rate, tax due would be $2,708, making the net $16,964.

WHAT ARE THE DISADVANTAGES OF TAX DEFERRED ANNUITIES?

There are two basic disadvantages: The first is that there are tax consequences to all withdrawals. Under current law, withdrawals are considered to come from accrued dividends and capital gains first and then principal, so that most, if not all, of your withdrawal will be taxable in the current year. Prior to August 1982, the law was different, and withdrawals were considered to be removal of principal first and dividends and capital gains last. These old annuities are still around and carry with them the same features.

The second disadvantage is one legislated by the federal government through the Tax Reform Act. Withdrawals are now treated very similarly to withdrawals from an IRA account or other pension account. Under age 59½, an individual would incur a 10 percent excise tax for removing any money from the annuity. Again, prior to August 1982, withdrawals from an annuity were permitted without any excise tax at any age.

WHAT ARE THE TAX IMPLICATIONS UNDER CURRENT LAW?

Any annuity purchased after August 1982 is presumed to withdraw earnings first; therefore withdrawals are fully taxable until all earnings are removed. That means that if you put $10,000 into an annuity and it grew to $20,000 as a result of capital growth and/or interest, your first

$10,000 worth of withdrawals would be considered 100 percent taxable at your current tax rate.

ONCE I PURCHASE AN ANNUITY, CAN I ADD ON TO MY INVESTMENT?

Annuities can be purchased in a flexible way, meaning you can make an initial deposit and then add on to it regularly. For example, you can buy an annuity with as little as $5,000 and add to it monthly, quarterly, or annually at will.

SUPPOSE I DON'T WANT TO ADD ON AND I JUST WANT TO MAKE ONE INVESTMENT?

Single premium deferred annuities, known as SPDAs, allow you to make a lump sum purchase and, in fact, do not permit add-ons.

HOW LONG WILL THE INTEREST RATE ON AN ANNUITY BE GUARANTEED?

Most annuities issued by insurance companies can guarantee a stated rate of interest for as little as three months and for as long as ten years. You can purchase an annuity, have a guaranteed interest rate for a stated period of time, and know exactly how many dollars will be there when it matures.

I DON'T LIKE THE IDEA OF INVESTING A LARGE SUM OF MONEY ALL IN ONE PLACE. WHAT INVESTMENT OPTIONS DO ANNUITIES OFFER?

There are many varieties of investment opportunities under the umbrella of deferred annuities. Some offer as many as 15 investment choices, ranging from money markets, corporate bond funds, government bond funds, growth and income stocks, international stocks, strategic allocation funds, etc. You can select the investment or combination of investments which suit your needs. For example, if you invest $12,000, you can specify that $4,000 go into money markets, $4,000 go into corporate bonds, and $4,000 go into growth and income stocks. Annuities of this kind also offer exchange privileges which allow you to change your selections at any time.

CAN I CONVERT AN EXISTING DEFERRED ANNUITY TO ONE THAT WILL GUARANTEE MONTHLY PAYMENTS, OR BUY A NEW ANNUITY THAT WILL GIVE ME MONTHLY PAYMENTS?

Yes. The conversion of deferred annuity funds or the purchase of an immediate annuity will result in guaranteed monthly payments for the rest of your life. Taking monthly payments (called annuitizing) can be an excellent way to spread out the tax consequences of an annuity since a portion of each payment is considered return of capital and is therefore tax free. How much of your payment is considered return of capital depends on the option you have chosen and the age you are when payments begin.

Since an annuity is often used in retirement planning, it can also be an excellent way to spread out the income you will have to take from all qualified accounts. These can be IRA accounts or Keogh accounts as well as 401K or other pension rollover dollars from employment pension plans. By combining all such accounts into an immediate annuity you can simplify distribution requirements and can guarantee a self-created monthly lifetime pension check.

WHAT KIND OF OPTIONS WILL AN IMMEDIATE ANNUITY GIVE ME?

All options provide monthly payments, paid to the annuitant (or to beneficiaries) for life, or for a certain stated period of time. For example, one option can be for "one life only" with no payments made to anyone other than the annuitant. Another option is "joint and survivor," which provides payments to the annuitant for his lifetime but also to a survivor beneficiary for life as well. Another option guarantees payments to heirs for 5, 10, or 20 years in the event the annuitant dies before this "certain period." The amount of the monthly payment is based on your option choice, gender, and age, and is based on actuarial tables. Once you select the option, it cannot be changed.

WHAT EXACTLY IS THE ONE-LIFE ONLY OPTION?

The purchase of an immediate one-life only annuity would guarantee lifetime payments to one person (the annuitant) only. There would be no guarantee to anyone else of any funds. Therefore, if you purchased a $100,000 annuity with this option and then died after receiving one, ten, or any number of checks, the balance of any funds remaining in your account would revert to the insurance company. In return for this risk, the monthly payment you receive would be considerably higher than one which gave anyone else additional benefits.

HOW DO I PREVENT MY INVESTMENT FROM REVERTING TO THE INSURANCE COMPANY?

You can choose one of the other options that would allow you to leave the remainder of your funds to another person, either for that person's lifetime (with a joint and survivor option), or for a specified period of time. For example, a 10-year period "certain and life" option means that for 10 years after the commencement of the pension either the annuitant or some other named beneficiary would receive the benefit. At the end of that period no further benefit would be provided.

CAN I CHANGE MY MIND AFTER I DECIDE WHAT KIND OF ANNUITY I WANT?

Unfortunately, an immediate annuity locks in the purchase payment to lifetime monthly payments and cannot be changed.

DO THE MONTHLY PAYMENTS VARY FROM ONE INSURANCE COMPANY TO ANOTHER?

The monthly payment is determined by the actuarial experience of the individual insurance company and varies from company to company. You should shop carefully and compare. For example, at age 65, you can purchase a $100,000 single lifetime annuity and receive as much as $884.38 per month or as little as $832 per month—depending on which company you choose. When you consider these payments over a lifetime, the difference can mean some serious money. A good consumer is an educated consumer who deals with facts and choices. If you are considering such a purchase, ask your insurance agent for his comparative shopping results— and make your own comparisons as well.

WHAT IS THE DISADVANTAGE OF AN IMMEDIATE ANNUITY IN TERMS OF SAVING ON TAXES?

If you are using qualified money, meaning retirement fund money, to buy the annuity, 100 percent of all income received from the annuity will be taxable to the annuitant or any beneficiary. Seeking tax advice from your accountant on this matter is very important.

IS IT TRUE THAT I CAN USE MY LIFE INSURANCE POLICY TO SAVE MONEY FOR RETIREMENT?

Life insurance policies that accumulate cash values serve dual purposes. The death benefit will provide funds directly to your beneficiaries or can be used to provide a retirement income source for them through the conversion of the benefit to an immediate annuity.

For you as the insured, the cash value can be borrowed out of your policy to provide income after retirement on a tax-favored basis. Unlike annuities, which for the most part produce taxable income as soon as you withdraw, life insurance funds withdrawn will be tax free and considered return of capital until all monies *invested* in the policy have been removed.

WON'T IT COST ME MONEY TO BORROW FROM MY LIFE INSURANCE?

Insurance companies have traditionally permitted the borrowing of cash values at very low rates of interest. Many permit loans which literally do not cost you money. For example, if your cash value life insurance policy is earning 7 percent interest you may be able to borrow at the same 7 percent interest. That would be a "wash" loan.

Some insurance companies will charge a differential of 1 percent. In other words, they may charge 8 percent interest for money that is earning 7 percent interest. Money borrowed in this fashion, of course, does not have to be repaid and is not considered a tax event until the policy is terminated. However, if you should die before the loan is repaid, the outstanding loan balance is deducted from the death benefit payment.

DOES THAT MEAN I CAN BORROW THE CASH VALUE, PERHAPS WITHOUT PAYING INTEREST AND WITHOUT PAYING TAXES ON THE MONEY I GET?

This is possible but there are two sets of rules that apply under the current tax laws.

First, life insurance policies are viewed as "insurance products" if premiums are paid in for a least seven years. If this is the case, then monies borrowed against the cash value are free of income tax as long as you maintain the policy. If the policy gets cashed out or "surrendered," you would then have taxable income on the difference between what you had paid in as premiums and the amount of money withdrawn from the policy.

Second, life insurance policies are considered "investment products" if premiums are paid in for less than seven years. Typically, this would be a single premium life policy. In this case, the rules that apply depend on when you purchased the policy. Prior to 1988, the old rules apply, meaning you could tap into the cash value of your policy with no tax consequence. After 1988, however, the rules changed. If the policy is considered an investment product, then the rules are similar to those for an annuity. Earnings on your premiums come out first as taxable income and then your premiums, or "principal."

CAN I USE LIFE INSURANCE TO SAVE FOR REASONS OTHER THAN RETIREMENT?

Yes, of course. The same process could be used for capital accumulated for education or any other reason.

WHAT ARE THE TAX CONSEQUENCES TO MY BENEFICIARY ON THE PROCEEDS OF LIFE INSURANCE?

For estate tax purposes, the proceeds from insurance may be included in the estate of the person who is deceased, unless that person relinquishes all rights relating to ownership. All amounts received by a beneficiary upon the insured's death are free from any current income taxes.

WHAT ABOUT INCOME TAX DUE ON ANNUITIES?

All annuities which accumulate tax-deferred will have income tax due on the difference between the capital investment and distribution value at death. That means the beneficiary will have to pay income tax on that distribution amount. This is one instance where Uncle Sam will get his due.

HOW DOES AN ANNUITY COMPARE TO OTHER INVESTMENTS?

A fixed annuity is comparable to a certificate of deposit or a bond in that there is a stated rate of return for a stated period of time with no possibility of loss to capital unless there is "premature" withdrawal of the funds.

A variable annuity is comparable to an investment in a mutual fund family. There are many different investment opportunities available in stocks, bonds, etc., with exchange privileges available as well.

The principal difference between annuity investment and other investments is the postponement of the obligation to pay taxes on earnings and the ability to convert the investment to lifetime income.

SECTION 5

SMART QUESTIONS TO ASK ABOUT SOPHISTICATED INVESTMENT OPTIONS

This section contains questions about six categories of investments that are definitely not advisable for the novice investor. Investments in real estate, rental equipment, foreign stocks and bonds, options, oil and gas ventures, and commodities, all take a thorough understanding of the individual laws and restrictions that apply, a well-devloped sense of the state of our present (and future) economy, and a fairly substantial amount of disposable income.

We included these categories, however, because we felt it important to cover as many investment choices as we could. You will probably have many more questions about each of these categories than we have supplied here. No matter how tempting an investment in any of

177

these categories appears, you can be sure it is very complicated—and risky.

You should ask questions of your broker, your tax advisor, your lawyer, and/or your financial planner before you make any investment decisions in these areas. Seek out people who have had a lot of experience in these type of investments, and question them about the results of their previous investment recommendations. Turn to the experts and *ask* until you are satisfied you have all the information you need.

SMART QUESTIONS TO ASK ABOUT INVESTMENTS IN REAL ESTATE

HOW CAN I FIGHT INFLATION BY INVESTING IN REAL ESTATE?

Real estate is viewed as an inflation-fighting investment because the prices historically mirror the rate of inflation. Real estate prices escalated during the early 1980s when inflation was 10 percent and more. By the same token, real estate prices declined during the recessionary periods. In effect, inflation-fighting investments are those that retain buying power.

Our tax laws have always favored the investor who purchases rental property, be it commercial, office space, or apartment housing. The primary advantage is that it not only permits the investor to deduct all expenses relating to the investment (such as interest on a mortgage, taxes, common charges, all improvements) but also allows for noncash out-of-pocket deductions (such as depreciation of the buildings involved as well as any capital improvements).This can be a very good tax strategy (techniques which help reduce tax burdens) for you, if you do not mind being a landlord.

WHAT IS DEPRECIATION?

Depreciation is the formula which allows you to deduct certain expenses over a period of time allowed by the IRS. For instance, depreciation of a capital improvement to a rental property, such as an updated kitchen, would be five years.

WHAT DOES IT MEAN TO BE OPERATING AT A TAX LOSS?

When expenses, including depreciation, are deducted from the rental income it is not unusual for property to be operating at a tax loss. If you are an active investor, meaning that you run the property (even with the help of a rental agent or management company), you can deduct any tax losses against any ordinary earned income on your federal and state tax return.

WHAT ARE THE ADVANTAGES AND DISADVANTAGES OF OPERATING AT A TAX LOSS?

The principal advantage of operating at a tax loss is that the loss may be on paper only. For example, if the property produces income of $6,000 per year and expenses average $4,000 per year, you actually have a positive cash flow of $2,000. However, if depreciation is $3,000 for the year, you have a tax loss of $1,000. If the property is in fact running a negative cash flow, with income of $6,000 and expenses of $7,000 before depreciation, the fact that depreciation increases your loss may be less important than the fact that running the property actually cost you $1,000 out-of-pocket.

HOW CAN I AVOID HAVING TO COLLECT RENT AND PAY EXPENSES?

You could hire a real estate management company to handle the rentals, repairs, and the paying of bills for you so that you have most of the advantages of owning real estate without most of the headaches.

CAN I INVEST IN REAL ESTATE WITHOUT ACTUALLY OWNING ANY?

The most common way to participate in the growth provided by real estate investment is through Real Estate Investment Trusts (REITs), Limited Partnerships, and Mutual Funds which participate in real estate investment. This is an excellent way to diversify your portfolio if you don't have a lot of money to invest and don't wish to be personally involved in running a property.

You could, for example, purchase 100 shares of a REIT for $10 a share. That way you would be investing in real estate for only $1,000, plus a brokerage commission charge of about $50. Mutual funds are available with a minimum initial investment of $1,000. Most limited partnerships have minimums of $2,000 for an IRA investment and $5,000 for a non-IRA investment.

HOW DOES AN REIT WORK?

A Real Estate Investment Trust is a publicly traded company which manages a portfolio of real estate. These investments can vary by kind, ranging from shopping centers and office buildings to apartment complexes, hotels, etc.

Some REITs, called Equity REITs, purchase properties and give shareholders any net income from rent on a regular basis, as well as capital gains when the buildings are sold. Others specialize in lending money, and are known as Mortgage REITs. These pass income on to shareholders from the mortgage payments made by building developers. There are also some REITs that are a blend of both equity and mortgage payments.

WHAT KIND OF INCOME CAN I EXPECT FROM A REIT?

The yield from a REIT depends on the kind of investments in its portfolio. If capital gain is the principal objective there may be very little, if any, income. The REIT may not produce any income if it contains mortgages which are in default, or income could be very high if a property is sold and a mortgage is repaid. REITs, therefore, are not a dependable, stable, income-producing investment. You should generally consider a REIT as a long-term capital gain producer and not as a source of income (although income may be a by-product).

WHICH TYPE OF REIT IS THE MOST RISKY?

All types of REITs can be risky, depending on the location of the properties and the manager of the portfolio. Overall, mortgage REITs are the least risky since they have income payments from mortgages which can ultimately be used as collateral in the event mortgage payments cannot be made.

I KNOW THAT THERE ARE TAX ADVANTAGES TO HOLDING REAL ESTATE. ARE THERE ANY TAX ADVANTAGES IN OWNING REITs?

No. All distributions made to shareholders are considered ordinary income, with the exception of capital gains, which are taxed as capital gains.

HOW DO MUTUAL FUNDS IN REAL ESTATE WORK?

Mutual fund investments in real estate are fairly new. Many fund managers take advantage of the cyclical nature of the real estate market. When there are economic downturns in a region of the country, that area often becomes overstocked with both apartments and commercial space. For example, the decline in automobile production has caused a surplus of real estate available in areas where layoffs have occurred. Property prices are then driven down as the supply becomes greater than the demand. Historically, these areas eventually become productive again and prices rise. Purchases of good properties at depressed prices can result in capital gain in a relatively short period of time.

Like any stock or bond fund, real estate mutual funds have active management. Properties in the fund may be bought and sold. Dollar-cost-averaging is possible since mutual funds permit additional investment and reinvest all dividends and gains. All distributions, reinvested or not, are taxable annually.

WHAT EXACTLY IS A LIMITED PARTNERSHIP?

Limited partnerships are in many respects similar to mutual funds. They allow the small investor to participate in investments which usually require personal, direct involvement and large down payments along with ongoing mortgage obligations.

For example, if you wanted to own rental real estate worth $100,000, you would deposit 10 percent ($10,000), carry a mortgage of $90,000, and provide management (either personally or through an agent) to rent and run the property. If you couldn't rent the property, you'd have to accept liability for expenses anyway.

As a limited partner, you could invest $5,000 in a portfolio of 20 to 40 properties, both residential and commercial, in as many as 20 to 40 different locations. Your liability is always limited to the amount of your investment (you might lose your investment, but you would not be liable for additional expenses). You cannot be asked for additional funds even if things are not going well.

In effect, you can join the large investors with a relatively small investment with no future obligations. Not only do you receive tax advantages, you also have the possibility that the value of the properties held will increase. The sale of the properties in the partnership could result in capital gain and increase your assets, which protects you against inflation.

WHAT ARE THE DISADVANTAGES OF A LIMITED PARTNERSHIP?

Limited partnerships offer almost no liquidity. If you should need cash, and want to sell your shares before the natural cycle of the partnership is over (for example after every property is sold), you may suffer large losses. Don't buy into a limited partnership unless you can accept its restrictions on liquidity. If you do have to sell, your losses may be 50 to 75 percent of your investment.

SMART QUESTIONS TO ASK ABOUT INVESTMENTS IN RENTAL EQUIPMENT

HOW CAN I INVEST IN RENTAL EQUIPMENT?

Most rental equipment investments involve limited partnerships. Almost any kind of equipment can be leased, including computers, production machinery services, cable television, medical technical support, and furniture.

The investment involves the leasing of equipment by the limited partnership to a company in return for lease payments. The equipment being leased is depreciated and therefore can provide income on a tax-favored basis since the losses generated by depreciation are used to wash out the rental income from lease payments.

HOW DOES DEPRECIATION WORK HERE?

The equipment being leased is being depreciated as the equipment is being used and loses resale value. The depreciation of the equipment is included in the calculation of the lease rental rates. A piece of equipment that depreciates quickly, such as a computer, will have a higher lease rate, relative to the cost of equipment, than a piece of equipment that has a much longer useful life, like an oil tanker. This depreciation does provide a tax deduction benefit to the partnership by sheltering from taxation a portion of the income from leases that would normally be subject to tax.

This tax-sheltered income represents to the investor, for tax purposes, a return of original invested principal. The longer the equipment is able to be leased, the more revenue is generated and the better the return. When the equipment is sold, a portion of your original investment is returned. Slowly depreciated equipment retains a higher percentage of original value than more quickly depreciated equipment.

HOW IS EQUIPMENT LEASING USED AS AN INFLATION HEDGE?

Lease rates reflect interest rates in the market place. When interest rates are high, lease rental rates are high. Conversely, when interest rates are low, lease interest rates are lower. Therefore, as an investor, you must be sure you understand that the rate or yield is not necessarily locked in for the entire length of the investment.

For the most part, leases run from one to seven years. As older leases are repaid and end, new leases are obtained at different rates. The yield can vary a great deal if interest rates vary a great deal, and that is really what makes it a hedge against inflation.

As inflation rates increase, the cost for new equipment escalates. While lease rates also increase, payments for leases can be more economical than payments for purchase. Outright purchase of heavy equipment usually requires large outlays of cash. In areas of high technology, with so many changes taking place so rapidly, companies are reluctant to make the investment in equipment which could be obsolete in a few years. Even though lease payments may be high, the company is not saddled with the equipment once the lease is over. On the other hand, the owner of the equipment can often rent the same "older" equipment to a company less technologically advanced.

SMART QUESTIONS TO ASK ABOUT FOREIGN STOCKS AND BONDS

WHAT ABOUT INVESTING BEYOND OUR COUNTRY'S BORDERS?

There is no doubt that we now live in a worldwide economy. What happens in one area of the world very much influences the economic life of another. There have always been foreign stocks available for American investors although possession of the certificate was never possible. Foreign securities issue American Depository Receipts (ADRs) and foreign stocks are held by brokerage houses in customer accounts as book entries.

Both stocks and debt securities of many countries are now available for purchase by American investors. It is, however, more difficult to obtain the same kinds of information about these securities that we can obtain about American securities. For the small investor, therefore, it is best to invest in mutual funds which have active management.

CAN I INVEST OVERSEAS WITH ONLY SMALL AMOUNTS OF MONEY?

There has been a large growth in the mutual funds around the area of foreign investing, although there are many different kinds of portfolios available, including the ones listed below:

Global funds: A global fund invests at least 25 percent of its portfolio in securities traded outside of the U.S. but may own U.S. securities as well.

International funds: An international fund invests its assets only in securities whose primary trading markets are outside of the U.S.

European funds: The European fund invests in equity securities whose primary trading markets or operations are concentrated in the European region. There are many funds which also single out a particular country, such as Germany, and isolate investments only to that country.

Pacific region funds: Those funds concentrate investments in equity securities whose primary trading markets or operations are in the Western Pacific basin, or in a single country within this region, such as Japan.

Latin America: This is an area of new interest in

the mutual fund industry, and funds are being created around investments in Latin America.

IT SOUNDS LIKE ALL THE OVERSEAS MUTUAL FUNDS I HEAR ABOUT ARE INVOLVED IN STOCKS. ARE THERE ANY THAT PROVIDE INCOME?

Yes, as a matter of fact, there are some very successful
bond funds, such as the Short World Income Fund which
invests in non-U.S. dollar and U.S. dollar bond instruments
with a very short average maturity or life. There are also
World Income General funds which invest in non-U.S. dollar
and U.S. dollar debt instruments like bonds with unspeci-
fied maturities or other income-producing securities.

SMART QUESTIONS TO ASK ABOUT OPTIONS

WHAT ARE OPTIONS?

Options are contractual agreements to buy or sell
stock and are actively traded on various exchanges. The
Chicago Board of Exchange (CBOE) is the most familiar.
However, options also trade on the New York, American,
Philadelphia, and Pacific exchanges. Most options are initially made for 30, 60, 90 days, or six months, and stipu-
late a price at which the holder of the option may
purchase or sell within that period of time. The standard
contract covers 100 shares.

WHAT KINDS OF STOCK OFFER OPTIONS?

Usually the more active and well-known stocks like IBM have options available, but some of the lesser-known stocks do as well.

WHAT IS A CALL OPTION?

A call option is a contract which allows the buyer to buy stock at a set price. It is used by a trader who expects the stock to rise in price before he exercises the option to buy the stock.

WHAT IS A PUT OPTION?

A put is a contract to sell stock at the contract or set price. It is used by a trader who expects the stock to fall in price, or an investor looking to protect gains on stocks currently held.

WHAT IS THE DIFFERENCE BETWEEN CALLS AND PUTS?

Effectively, one works exactly the reverse of the other. One gives the investor the right to buy at a given price and the other the right to sell at a given price.

WHAT IS A STRADDLE?

A straddle entitles the holder to either a put or a call. It is a speculative position and is used by the investor who expects real fluctuation in the market but is not sure whether the major change will be up or down.

WHO SHOULD USE OPTIONS AS AN INVESTMENT TECHNIQUE?

For the most part, purchasers of options are speculators who want to take large positions in a stock with a small amount of money. Statistically, the majority do not profit from their use. It can be and frequently is used as a defensive strategy by investors trying to protect their portfolios from dramatic losses.

DOES THE USE OF OPTIONS SERVE ANY OTHER PURPOSE?

It is possible to use options to create income for the investor. For example, an investor who sells calls receives money in exchange for his willingness to give up his stock at a given price. Of course, if the market moves in his favor, the option will expire and he can keep the money he received and the stock. There are investors who use this strategy. The option premium can be as much as 10 to 15 percent of the price of the stock. In addition, you are entitled to any dividends on the underlying stock as well if you own the stock.

HOW DO OPTIONS PROTECT YOU AGAINST LOSS?

Specifically, a put option allows you to sell stock to an investor who purchases the contract at a set price. Whether the stock price rises or falls is of no consequence since the price is predetermined. The stock can be "put" to the buyer at the price on the contract any time during the contract period. You can in that way lock in a profit on your stock. Let's assume you paid $50 a share and want to lock in a $10 per share profit. If you sell an option at $60 a share, you have locked in that profit. Of course, the stock can still go up to $75, and you would be locked in to selling at $60.

WHAT IS THE DIFFERENCE BETWEEN COVERED AND UNCOVERED CALL OPTIONS?

A covered option means the seller actually owns the stock he has promised to deliver at a set price before the contract expires. He is entitled to any dividends and rights as a stockholder during the contract period. An uncovered option means the seller does not own the stock and would have to buy the stock at whatever price it was selling at in order to meet his obligation to deliver. This is a far riskier strategy than a covered option.

SMART QUESTIONS TO ASK ABOUT OIL AND GAS VENTURES

HOW CAN I GET INTO EXPLORATION OF OIL AND GAS?

The most popular way to invest directly in oil and gas is through the limited partnership. This investment vehicle gives you benefits without management responsibilities or financial responsibilities. Your liability is limited to the amount you have invested.

The partnership may invest in developmental wells, those that are drilled in areas where oil has already been found. These are more predictable than exploratory wells, which are dug in areas where geologists believe oil or gas can be found, but where none have been found yet.

ARE EXPLORATORY WELLS A RISKY INVESTMENT?

This is an area of investment which can be highly risky. It is estimated that only one in fifteen wildcat wells results in even a small oil field. Not only does your financial success depend on finding oil, but it also depends on the price you receive when selling it. One alternative is to buy stock in a major oil company. The company explores for oil and gas and you can participate as a shareholder in the corporation.

ARE LIMITED PARTNERSHIPS IN OIL AND GAS RISKY?

Not all limited partnerships are created equal. Oil and gas drilling programs have been offered to investors for many years, but usually only the wealthiest individuals or institutions were able to participate. The higher tax bracket investor found this kind of program to be an excellent tax shelter, and if oil and gas were discovered, the rewards of the investment could be substantial.

Partnerships created to produce income generated by existing oil and gas properties are less risky. They, in effect, create a mutual fund of various already producing oil and natural gas properties for the income or profit they can generate as long as production continues.

The real danger in all oil and gas programs is the substantial fluctuation in the price of oil and gas in the past few years. With the ongoing uncertainty in the Middle East, foreign production is another unpredictable part of the equation. Therefore, even income partnerships can be somewhat risky.

WHAT IS MY LIABILITY AS A LIMITED PARTNER?

Your liability is limited to the amount of your investment. You cannot be asked to assume any responsibility for additional funds which may be needed to operate the partnership or for any other reason. It is the General Partner who assumes all the liability.

ARE THERE TAX ADVANTAGES TO JOINING A LIMITED PARTNERSHIP?

Deductions from gross income of intangible drilling costs (IDCs) and depletion allowance can make the investment an attractive tax shelter. Limited partnerships, registered with the SEC, have been and continue to be attractive to the public as a way of investing in oil and gas.

WHAT IS A TAX SHELTER?

The term tax shelter refers to those investments that enjoy certain tax benefits. For example, when you own rental real estate or equipment, you are permitted to "write off" or depreciate certain physical property over a scheduled number of years. Suppose you have renovated the kitchen of your rental apartment for a cost of $15,000 on a property which allows for a five-year depreciation schedule. You would therefore be able to take a "loss" of $3,000 per year, deducted against the income from the rental property. Items like depreciation in oil and gas programs are noncash items which "shelter" income by providing deductions against it.

SMART QUESTIONS TO ASK ABOUT COMMODITIES FUTURES

WHAT ARE BASIC COMMODITIES FUTURES?

Future contracts are written in hopes of profiting from price changes in corn, oats, wheat, soybeans, copper, silver, platinum, and the much discussed pork bellies, along with many more.

WHAT EXACTLY IS A FUTURES CONTRACT?

It is an agreement to buy or sell a commodity at a stated price on a specified future date. Contracts are usually "closed out" before the maturity date so that the commodity itself never changes hands.

HOW DOES THIS WORK?

For example, suppose a speculator thought the price of corn was going up. He buys a futures contract which will allow him to buy 10,000 bushels of corn for delivery in December at $3 a bushel. Suppose a month later the price of corn for delivery in December is $3.25 a bushel. If he closes out or sells his contract, he could realize a profit of $2,500 (10,000 x $.25). Suppose the price goes down to $2.75 a bushel instead? If the price stays down into December, the speculator will lose all of his investment.

HOW MUCH OF A RISK IS COMMODITY FUTURES TRADING?

Probably one of the highest, since statistically speculators lose 75 to 80 percent of the time. These are super risky investments and do not belong in the average portfolio.

CONCLUSION

TEN KEY POINTS ABOUT YOU AND YOUR STOCKBROKER

1. YOU CAN, AND MUST, TAKE RESPONSIBILITY FOR YOUR OWN INVESTMENT "HEALTH" AND WELL-BEING.
This doesn't mean you have to become your own broker or financial planner or make all decisions by yourself. It does mean that you have to make informed choices about the brokers, financial advisors, and investment options you choose.

2. STAND UP FOR YOUR RIGHT TO ASK QUESTIONS.
You have to be persistent. A broker may be busy, or may not be prepared to answer all your questions.

However, brokers are taught to ask questions—and you may have to remind your broker that he is not the only one who can ask them.

3. THE ONLY WAY TO GET THE INFORMATION YOU NEED IS BY ASKING QUESTIONS.

Don't be afraid to admit you don't know. Great inventions and scientific discoveries were made by people who "didn't know." They admitted to the world they didn't know all the answers; then they asked questions, questions, and more questions, until they found the answers they needed.

4. DISCOVER YOUR OPTIONS.

Options give you control over any situation. Never do anything (or refrain from doing anything), just because your broker said so. Find out what your choices are, then make your decision.

5. KNOWLEDGE REDUCES FEAR AND ANXIETY.

It's not what we know that scares us, it's what we don't know. Decisions that involve present and future finances can be very stressful, for yourself and for your family. You don't want to waste your strength and energy on imaginary or unnecessary concerns.

6. NEVER ASSUME.

Don't assume that you have all the information you need. A broker may have given similar investment advice to 2,000 other people—but forget to give you one vital piece of information. Don't assume something is right for you just because a broker says it's so. Think about what you're doing, and make the broker think as well!

7. DON'T ACCEPT AN EASY ANSWER. PROBE AND CLARIFY.

Little children do this automatically. Answer a question and they'll come back with a "WHY?" every time. You should do the same. You want to be sure you understand everything that's going on, and that you are getting your money's worth for any services rendered.

8. A BROKER IS JUST A HUMAN BEING.

No matter how intimidating, aggressive, or knowledgeable she may seem, a broker really is just a human being. That means she can make human mistakes. She can also be warm, sympathetic, and understanding. Let her know what you need, and how she can help you.

9. BUILD A ONE-ON-ONE RELATIONSHIP WITH YOUR BROKER.

You don't have to become best friends. Asking questions sets up an immediate rapport with the broker. The broker's attitudes, as well as his answers, will give you important clues about his background and personality—and help you make a choice that is right for you.

Your questioning attitude lets him know that you're special, and that you intend to establish a

partnership with him concerning all your investment
dealings.

10. ASK SMART QUESTIONS. ASK SMART QUES-
TIONS. ASK MORE SMART QUESTIONS.

INDEX